Christian Faith

and the

Question of History

NORMAN PITTENGER

Christian Faith
and the
Question of History

FORTRESS PRESS

Philadelphia

Library of Congress Catalog Card Number 73-79353

ISBN 0-8006-1057-1

3785C73   Printed in U.S.A.   1-1057

Table of Contents

Preface

The question of history and Christian faith has lately engaged the attention of theologians, but to the best of my knowledge, none of these (with the exception of Van Harvey, in incidental references) seems to have approached the matter from the position of an avowed supporter of "process thought." For the most part, writers have looked at the entire issue from what may be called a "biblical theological" position. It is my conviction that such a look needs to be supplemented by the insights which we owe to the "process" conceptuality which currently is increasingly being accepted by many Christian thinkers. In this book, I have tried to take this approach.

The first chapter considers the ways in which Christianity has shown itself to be an historical religion. The succeeding chapters discuss what may be termed the general biblical position in relation to history; the various contexts in which the term "history" currently is being used by secular as well as religious writers; the way in which the Christian community has embodied and expressed its historical reality and how the Christian believer enters into and appropriates this history; the question of miracle as it poses itself to us in historical terms; and finally, the fulfillment of history in God. This is an enormous program and we shall be able to do little more than make suggestions which may prove interesting and, hopefully, useful.

Two prefatory comments may be helpful. First, I have purposely avoided loading the book with extended "scholarly apparatus," since I am trying to reach a wider audience and especially those who as laymen have no concern for such technical exhibitionism. Any scholars who may do me the honor of reading the book will know how indebted I am to much that has been written lately on the subject. Second, the material in this book originally were lectures given at the Divinity School of Vanderbilt University, St. Luke's School of Theology at the University of the South, and at conferences and clergy gatherings during 1972. I delivered these lectures as a Christian theologian who is a member of the Anglican Communion—the Episcopal Church or the Church of England. This will explain some of the references and will do something to indicate my own particular way of being a Christian. But I have been pleased to find that Christians of other denominational affiliations, including Roman Catholics, Lutherans, Presbyterians, and Disciples of Christ have been able to accept what I have said as being broadly Christian and not specifically Anglican.

The lectures were prepared in Rome in the summer of 1971 and later revised at King's College, Cambridge, where I have the honor of being a Senior Resident, after having taught for more than thirty years at the General Seminary in New York.

I am indebted to my old friends, Dean Walter Harrelson of Vanderbilt and Dean George Alexander of Sewanee, for the opportunity to speak at their schools in February 1972. I am also grateful to the large audiences that attended the lectures and for the interesting discussion periods that followed.

King's College   Norman Pittenger
Cambridge, England

CHAPTER 1

The Question Before Us

The purpose of this book is to discuss the question of the relationship of Christian faith and history. The problem is no new one, but in recent years it has received a considerable amount of attention, especially because of a change in the understanding of the nature of history. In an older day, history was taken to mean simply the study of the past; more recently, history has been interpreted as having to do with the past known, accepted, and effective in the present. That this view has a significant bearing upon Christian faith ought to be apparent. On the other hand, biblical scholars, in the past twenty-five years, have concerned themselves more and more with the way in which the Jewish mind understood its historical background; here, once again, the bearing of this upon Christian faith is clear.

But the present essay is written from a particular point of view which, in my judgment, can be of very great assistance in our consideration of the question of faith and history. That point of view is the conceptuality commonly known these days as "process thought," associated with the work of Alfred North Whitehead and those who in one way or another are his disciples. We shall see in more detail the various aspects of this conceptuality which are relevant to our present task. It will suffice at this point simply to stress the three factors which are central in process thought today. First is the vision of the total cosmos as an evolutionary movement; it is "in process." Second is the way in which everything in the cosmos, including human history and experience, must be seen as interrelated and interpenetrative—hence as organismic or societal. Third is the refusal to allow a sharp dichotomy between the natural processes and historical developments, but on the contrary to insist on a radical historicization of nature and a disclosure in historical existence of what basically is going on in the cosmos as a whole. Each of these factors has its relevance to the problem with which this book is concerned.

The word "history" with its adjective "historical" has a certain ambiguity. When these terms have been applied to Christianity, some have thought that the point was that in Christian faith we look back across the centuries to an "historical" figure, Jesus of Nazareth, who lived at a certain time and place, whose existence as such a figure is integral to the entire Christian enterprise since the specifically Christian faith is directed toward that man about whom we must claim adequate knowledge as a person and who did in fact live there and then. But others have assumed that when we speak of Christianity as historical we are not merely referring to events which may be placed and dated but are also talking about an "historical community" which is rooted in the on-going life of men and whose message (whatever we may be able to say, or not say, about the past event) is spoken to men in their own given historical situations. There are other possible meanings, too. German scholars have made much of the distinction between *historie* and *geschichte*: the record of the past events taken to be factual, on the one hand, and the interpreted or felt significance of events in human apprehension through faith, on the other.

One day many years ago, in a seminar that I was conducting, I noted on a sheet of paper thirteen different meanings that had been given the word "history" during the course of a two-hour discussion. These ranged from the simple writing of history as chronicle or annal to the sophisticated idea of history as an entrance into the spirit of past events through what was an almost idealistic identification of thought and reality. What are we to understand by this term "history?"

It is my contention that one of the chief contributions of process thought is its capacity to illuminate the term "history." So far as I am aware, very few if any treatments of the question now before us have made much use of that conceptuality. Some have been touched by it, to be sure; but a single-minded consideration of the issue from that perspective has yet to be published. I dare not claim that this book will supply this need, but I trust that it will be an essay in that direction. And one thing will become very clear, as I see it. The sharp line which it has been fashionable to draw between nature and history is not only intolerable to our minds but impossible when we take account of the facts. Certain biblical theologians have ventured the assertion that the Scriptures are strictly "historical," in utter contrast with "culture-religions" which have to do with supposed recurrences in the realm of nature and have no room for the specificity of given historical events. I wish to combat this position, not because I deny that there are some religions which thus lack any sense of history but because I believe that the very Scriptures to which appeal is made will not permit the dichotomy which is proposed. The Bible has much to say about nature, whose author is the same God as he who is active in events styled historical.

Furthermore, many of those who talk in this fashion are captive to a nineteenth-century view of the natural world in which evolutionary change was assumed to mean only various different configurations of bits of matter in motion, with no possible genuine novelty; it was indeed a matter of "recurrence" with slight or great complications but with nothing new in the changing cosmos. If we interpret nature, as modern evolutionary thinking says we must—as epigenetic—with emergence of real novelty as the process moves onward, we must see that nature too has a history. That is, it is getting somewhere, it is producing novel emergents, and it is not only dynamic rather than machine-like but is also (in at least one sense) a living and not a dead enterprise. Not merely must we grant that all historical events have a geographical setting and context; we must also see that nature itself is event-full.

One of the major achievements of New Testament scholarship during the past century has been its demonstration that the Jesus who is believed by Christians to be in some profound sense divine was also, and most certainly, an historical human being who, like all other men, lived at a particular time and in a particular place. He shared in the thought and he participated in the religious life of his own people. Nobody today would think for a moment that Jesus' divinity—whatever that may be taken to mean—requires a denial or disregard of his full and complete humanity.

But at the same time, the very critical study which has assured us of this human reality of Jesus has also—and especially in more recent years—been very clear that our way of getting at that figure must be through the witness of men who believed Jesus to be their lord and master and were sure of the divine activity which was at work within him. We do not have any knowledge of a Jesus who is not already accepted as in some sense divine. The documents that tell us about him as an historical, human figure, in the ordinary meaning of those words, are the products of a community that centered its faith in him. Hence, the documents are colored by the community's beliefs, as well as by their religious practices; and we are unable to get behind this witness to a neutral sort of figure, discovering the sheer facts of his life as it was lived in Palestine in the first third of the first century of our era.

These two developments—the assurance of a genuine humanity at a point of history and the witness given to that humanity by a community that, in its stories, was seeking to speak "from faith to faith"—have produced a situation which is both difficult and liable to lead to much misunderstanding. The problem is not only for the theologian; knowledge of its existence may have serious consequences for simple believers. If this is the only way in which we can get at the Jesus who is believed to be Lord, have we any security whatsoever in that faith in him as in some significant sense both an act of God in the realm of human affairs and the savior of men? Are we not in danger of believing in Jesus as no more than the central figure in a religious myth? The myth may be very important; it may even tell us the truth about our human condition and about our relationship to God. But if it is only a myth, in the meaning commonly given that term, one among other possible mythological constructions, has it not lost its cutting edge? Have we any compelling reason to choose this myth rather than some other?

In the way in which I have just phrased the matter, following the thought of the ordinary Christian believer, there is obviously a misrepresentation of the situation. For instance, the significance of the word "myth" needs to be examined. Further, the subtleties of New Testament study have not been adequately represented. Nor has the sense in which all historical material, when it is more than a list of dates, must of necessity include some degree of interpretation, received its proper attention. Nonetheless, we cannot do other than sympathize with men or women who talk in that fashion, for they feel that something which is not only important but actually crucial in their faith has been threatened. They wonder if the faith by which they have lived can stand secure, when doubt is expressed as to the accuracy of the details of the gospel narratives. They seem, sometimes, to think that "they have taken away my Lord" and they do not know where they can go to find him again. Is there any way in which such people can be assisted, without at the same time retreating into a variety of fundamentalism or theological obscurantism?

The first point which I wish to urge is that we have absolutely no reason to assume that the whole story of the beginnings of Christianity in the concrete existence of the man Jesus has been put into doubt. While we dare not minimize the problem, nor try to evade what Paul Tillich rightly styled "our time of trouble" caused for Christian faith by the results of scientific New Testament study, we need not succumb to the opposite temptation. No responsible New Testament scholar and no responsible secular historian is likely, these days, to think that the fact of Jesus Christ, as a genuine personage in the realm of events, is not at least as well certified to us as most other facts coming from the remote past. And that, in itself, is worth our remembering.

The old "Christ-myth" school, associated with such names as W. B. Smith, is entirely dead, despite a few uninformed attempts in recent years to resurrect it. Whatever else may be said about Jesus of Nazareth, he is not the creation of religious-minded fanatics of the first century, fashioned as a lay figure upon which to attach a number of divine appellations and use as a symbol for religious truths prevalent in certain quarters of the Greco-Roman world. The experts in New Testament study, including Alfred Loisy in the earlier decades of the century and Rudolf Bultmann in our own time, have made it clear that the only viable explanation of the preaching about Jesus is the factual veracity of a life which was actually lived in Palestine. We may not know as much as we might wish about that life; certainly we are not in a position to draw the picture of Jesus' "personality"—in the fashion of nineteenth-century writers who delighted in making Jesus the hero of a psychological romance, tracing the development of his self-consciousness and portraying the ways in which he realized and effected his vocation. But the most radical scholars these days are no supporters of a "myth" theory in the older sense. Bultmann, commonly regarded as the most skeptical, speaks with confidence about Jesus, his prophetic outlook, and his obedience to what he regarded as the divine will for him. The most primitive material, even if it comes to us as seen through "the eyes of faith" and in terms of a *kerygma* or preaching by the Christian community, is trustworthy at least to the extent of talking about a real man. Thus, in the vulgar sense of the word "myth," the Jesus of history is not portrayed as a mythical figure, preaching or teaching, and who managed in some strange way to convert large numbers of people.

We need also to recognize that the word "myth" can be much misunderstood. As it is commonly used, it suggests a "fairy-tale," created more or less *ad hoc* with no real basis in facts which, in principle, some observer might have noted and reported had he been present. But the word—or its Greek equivalent—is used by Plato to suggest "a likely tale," without any judgment as to the factuality of the incidents which it includes. In this sense, a story which is told to prove or demonstrate a significant truth or to illustrate vividly how things go in the world, might very well have some factual basis. It would be called a "myth" precisely because it possessed such an illustrative, demonstrative, or evocative quality. Or again, as the word is used by Bultmann, it can mean the portrayal of divine-human relationships in terms that are drawn from the experience of men in this world. How otherwise could men portray something so intangible as God's way with his creatures than by the use of known relationships, experiences, and feelings in the realm of human affairs? This is "talking about the other world and its contacts with us, in the language of this world and our human contacts," as it has been phrased. In that case, to "demythologize" the story of Jesus (as Bultmann proposes, although the word "demythologize" is not the exact English equivalent to what his German intends) is essentially to get at the basic truth which in such "mythological" terms is being said, without for a moment necessarily denying that there are genuine historical elements included in the given representation.

It is also possible to use the word in a wide sense to indicate that there is more significance in a given event than the certain, factual event or happening. Thus Tennyson in his *In Memoriam* wrote about the portrayal of Christ in the gospels, in words that have become well-known:

> For wisdom dealt with mortal powers
> Where truth in closest words must fail,

> When truth embodied in a tale
> Shall enter in at lowly doors.

> And so the Word had breath and wrought
> With human hands the creed of creeds.

7

Tennyson's point is that because men do not normally think conceptually or in strictly intellectual categories—but more often in terms of images and pictures—God's nature and purpose, God's word disclosed to his human children, was embodied for them and wrought out before them and in their midst in a "tale" (a "myth," we may say) which they could understand and by which they could be grasped. In this way alone could true "Wisdom" find a way to deal "with mortal powers" and the truth about his nature and purpose, given focus in a human life, "enter in at lowly doors." In effect, this suggests to us something that the very learned often forget: namely, that not only children but mature men and women are much more likely to respond to and find value in a story told them than in a set of propositions phrased in abstract philosophical idiom.

Because of the confusion over the word "myth," I ventured to suggest as long ago as 1959, in my christological study *The Word Incarnate,* that it would be much simpler if we did not use that term when we are speaking about what we believe to be grounded in fact. At the same time I recognized that the kind of language that we must use when the event is believed to have special and determinative significance is "mythological" in quality, that is, language which is metaphorical or poetical, rather than literal. I both understand and appreciate the criticisms that some have made of this suggestion, but I am still convinced that it was sound. We shall have more to say about this matter in a later context; my reason for mentioning it here is to indicate that many of those who today speak of the Christian story as "myth" do not intend, in any way, to deny the genuine factual base of the gospel material and thus to make the story into an edifying "fairy-tale."

Finally, we need to understand better what has taken place with respect to our knowledge about the historical (again in the ordinary sense of factual) Jesus. The change has been in the stance which we must occupy; or, to phrase it otherwise, it is a difference in our mode of coming to knowledge about him. We have been brought to recognize that the gospel narratives are not to be read as if they were straight biography. Nor are they of the nature of newspaper reporting. In the first flush of success in New Testament scholarship, many believed that it was now possible in some direct fashion to get to the Jesus who walked and taught and acted in Palestine, as we might do with material written about some contemporary. It was as if observers and auditors had been equipped with cameras and microphones so that what they tell us is an exact account of what was seen and heard. But a moment's thought shows how absurd this idea is. Even in the days when scholars thought that the material had been written at a very early date by eyewitnesses or those to whom eye-witnesses had talked, they were obliged to recognize the modifications that had occurred in the successive stages of copying and editing. It was a great gain when the form-critical school demonstrated, by the use of methods which had been successful in handling other ancient writing, that there had been a long period of oral transmission, perhaps lasting as long as twenty to fifty years, during which short accounts of various types had been repeated within the Christian community as part of the normal teaching mission and as a method by which the impact of the Lord and the demands which he made were imparted to catechumens and to established believers. In such a process some degree of modification was inevitable; and the critics worked out certain principles which would help to show how and why the modifications had taken place.

Today, confidence in the principles thus enunciated is somewhat shaken, although their usefulness is not denied. The new redaction-criticism, stressing the part played by the editors of the documents in stringing together material familiar to them and seeking in this arrangement to convey theological and moral convictions which they believed important, has come forward to reaffirm the indirection of the gospel narratives and to show that direct access to the historical Jesus is not possible. But this does not mean that we cannot have confidence in the general veracity of the image of Jesus in the collected material nor make it absurd to think that the theological and moral convictions of the redactors were created out of thin air. Rather, these convictions rested on a certainty that they were treating of something that had indeed taken place. They were trying to communicate what this happening meant; they were not unconcerned about its ever having occurred at all.

In other words, modern New Testament scholarship has not resulted in the complete dehistoricization of Jesus nor in the denial to us today of some valid information about him. We do not have precise details which we can accept as they stand; certainly we do not find ourselves in the pleasant position of reading the gospels as if they were straight reporting. On the other hand, we have every reason to suppose that the general impression we receive from reading the first three (or synoptic) gospels is trustworthy. We may also include the fourth gospel, St. John, since it is now pretty certainly demonstrated that the compiler of that gospel had access to traditional material or to a tradition different from those available to the synoptic editors; he handled it in a different, perhaps more imaginative, fashion, but he was not engaging in fanciful fabrication of a figure for whom there was no genuine factual basis. In the gospels as a whole there is a portrayal of one who speaks and acts with a consistency of purpose which would hardly be possible if he were "made up out of the whole cloth."

Jesus may not have said or done exactly this or that which is reported of him in the gospels. But he was this sort of man. We may take some examples. He may not, probably did not, claim to be the Messiah, although the material which we possess appears to make this claim on his behalf and to put the statement of it in his own mouth. On the other hand, his authoritative representation of what he took to be his heavenly Father's will and his demand for a response to that representation are written all over the gospels; there is no reason to doubt the accuracy of this remembrance and indeed many spokesmen for what is called "the new quest for the historical Jesus" place their chief stress on this.

It is not difficult to see how in later years the Messianic claims could be put in his mouth, since the Messiah was thought to be exactly that one of whom such statements could be made. Or, to take another example, Jesus may not have stilled a storm on the Lake of Galilee; probably he did not. But almost certainly the story rests upon some incident which has been much heightened in the telling. The exact details of that incident we do not know, but very likely there was some occasion when during bad weather on the lake Jesus strengthened the faith of his friends. His authority and commanding presence were remembered. The oral tradition, building upon such reminiscence, interpreted it in line with Jewish thinking and came to tell of incidents or an incident when during a wild storm Jesus had spoken words with an authoritative quality.

The important thing is to see that each incident is considered on its own merits, with due regard for the peculiar characteristics which it shows and with respect to its congruity with the more general picture of the character and attitude of Jesus. The result will be that the general picture will not, of course, guarantee the historicity of the several narratives; but it will rest upon what has been styled "the overall impression of Jesus" which the whole gospel material presents to us. That general picture has every claim to be both credible and reliable.

This stance or mode of approach to the narratives means that we must look at the gospels in a different way from that which has been conventional in Christian circles for a very long time. The stories are told by those who believed in Jesus, were entirely committed to him, and wished to bring others to share the new life which they knew from discipleship to him in the community of Christian faith, worship, and action. The stories are told to those who are also members of the community or who are being brought into the community through their response to the proclamation of Jesus as God's Messiah, the Savior of Men, and the act of God in self-disclosure to his children. We must read the gospels as if they were "letters of commendation," written to

11

bring to our notice and urge for our acceptance the person about whom they tell. Like most such letters, as anyone who has written or received them knows very well, they may not always be exact in detail and they are inclined to heighten the commendatory element—not because they are lying about the facts but because they wish to make very clear the high regard in which the person being commended is held by the writer. This does not suggest that the whole is a fanciful tale of an edifying or inspiring sort. It has to do with something and with someone dated and placed in a given time and nation; it is about a human figure who lived and taught and acted and died—and who was firmly believed, by those who had known him, to be in some way victorious through death and over death. His dying had been vindicated to their faith by experiences which they describe in the odd language (to us, anyway) of resurrection appearances of the Lord to his disciples. About this we must speak in a later chapter. The point here is that for those who gave us the stories about Jesus, this was a matter firmly anchored in the realm which they regarded as genuine event.

Thus we can readily see that the first and most obvious meaning of calling the Christian faith historical is the stress on the human figure of Jesus as a genuine reality in that realm of event. In the first century of our era a life was lived, in all its richness, which indubitably is a matter of fact. If this were not so, the entire Christian enterprise would collapse, since (as Professor A. E. Taylor once remarked) it might otherwise be a symbol of what is "most dreadfully *untrue*." Associated with this sense of the historical is another, closely related. Christianity is a "founded" religion in the sense that it looks back to such an historical existence and regards itself as built upon it. Christianity is distinctive in that it does not take Jesus himself to be the founder of a religion, like Mohammed. So far as Jesus' teaching goes, he made no such pretensions. He regarded himself as one who spoke and acted as a faithful Jew; doubtless he would have been horrified if anybody had thought that he was establishing a new faith—on the contrary he was "fulfilling," bringing out the true meaning of, the Jewish faith which he inherited and accepted. Yet in this zealous concern for the reform and purification of Jewish religious life, bringing it into conformity with what he knew of God's intention for the "chosen people" and for the world, a community came into existence. Jesus was not its founder; it was founded (that is, based and centered) on him. Or as the hymn puts it, "the Church's one *foundation* is Jesus Christ, her Lord."

These two associated meanings of historicity are plain enough. There is another sense, however, which is not always quite so clearly understood. This other sense is of great importance for us, as we shall see; it has to do with Christianity as a positive religion, to use the anthropologists' term. Unlike those religions which celebrate the seasons or which have their chief interest in natural phenomena, Christianity is historically transmitted and historically shared in an historical society which has an historical continuity. I have repeated the adjective "historical" here because it helps to make my point. Judaism, Islam, and Buddhism are also examples of historical religions in this sense of positive faiths with a communal transmission. Each of them is conveyed by an organized group of men and women who have developed specific structures, who engage in specific activities, and who have been incorporated into a society that is ploughed into the eventful continuity of the human race. This meaning of historical is better understood in the so-called catholic churches than it has been in Protestant or Reformed circles, although the fact of it has been as real in the latter as in the former. In recent years, we must also note, theologians and church leaders in the Protestant or Reformed churches have been particularly emphatic on the point. They have rediscovered the reality of their historicity, in this particular meaning of the word, and it has produced an increased "church-consciousness" and a lively concern for the reintegration of all Christians into a community whose communal nature, both through the centuries and across the world, will be plainly visible to everyone.

Before we turn to some of the issues which have been raised, however, we must say something about the conceptuality which provides for this book its perspective on the faith. One way of getting at this conceptuality is by considering the relation of history and nature. Is history sharply cut off from the world of natural occurrences so that the latter provides only a stage upon which events are enacted? Or is there a much more intimate relationship here? The answer which must be given, in my judgment, is that there is indeed an intimate relationship. History has a geography; events emerge from the natural order and are revelatory of what is going on, invisibly most of the time, in the cosmos as a whole. The conceptuality known as process thought is insistent upon precisely this point.

An increasing number of responsible thinkers, keenly aware of the contribution of scientific research to our knowledge but also sensitive to the aesthetic and moral aspects of human experience as well as to the fact of religion as a universal human phenomenon, have come to believe that the world in which we live, and of which we are a part, is no collection of things, each of them located at a specific place and time, but is an on-going process in which energy-events (as they have been called) are the basic elements. The world is a dynamic movement in which occurrences or events take place, each of them actualizing in greater or lesser degree of adequacy the potentialities which are theirs. This movement in each instance is *from* some "initial aim" which is supplied by God from among the infinite number of possibilities in the continuum of possibilities which exist abstractly ("ideal objects," in Whitehead's phrase); it is *through a* series of decisions in which impinging elements of experience are accepted or rejected and in which there is a continual mutual grasping of the other occasions or events in the world; and it is *toward* the satisfaction or fulfillment of this "aim" which has been adopted as its own ("the initial aim" has been made the "subjective aim" of the occasion). In such a world there is an interrelationship of each event with all other events, either vividly or dimly, consciously or

14

unconsciously, so that the total on-going process is societal or organismic in nature. Here is no machine grinding on without goals; here is no repetitive pattern in which nothing really happens. Happening is in fact the basic ingredient of the whole enterprise of creative advance. Furthermore, there is the emergence again and again of something genuinely new, in particular places and at particular moments. Such novelty is not by intrusion from outside the process since there is no "outside" about which we can talk meaningfully. It is the consequence of increasing complexity of the organisms or events in question, using the given "stuff" of the past in a novel way and hence producing a novel result. And the whole is within a greater and all-encompassing continuity of creative advance of which God is the infinite resource, the chief causative agency, and the supreme recipient or affective end.

I have summarized briefly and in very abstract language a position which was developed with much precision by Alfred North Whitehead in a number of highly important works of which the most significant are probably *Science and the Modern World, Adventures of Ideas,* and *Process and Reality.* This general conceptuality was applied by Whitehead to religion in his Lowell Lectures, *Religion in the Making.* It is unnecessary to mention here the names of living authors and their writings, which follow this process line; a discussion with bibliography may be found in *Process Thought and Christian Faith,* in which I have attempted an introduction to the subject, and in the booklet *Alfred North Whitehead,* published in the series "Makers of Contemporary Theology."

Our concern in the present essay is not with the details of the process position. It is with what I style the "historicization of nature" which is integral to this conceptuality. I believe that this significant aspect of process thought can help us to overcome the supposed dualism between nature and history and in this way give us a better grasp of the way in which history illuminates the whole creative advance. Furthermore, I believe that in this fashion we can come to a sound view of the wholeness of human experience. For a Christian (and for a Jew also) this is especially important since the Bible refuses to set up a dualism here; it finds man a whole entity in an historical movement which is part of a process indwelt and activated at every point by God.

When we look at the world of nature and observe what seem its stabilities, on the one hand, and its repetitive patterns, on the other, we may very well assume that it is dead, that what has been, will be, and that the round of the seasons stands as a symbol of an almost mechanical system which will go on as long as creation lasts. But science today does not speak in this fashion. And a process thinker finds it incredible that anyone should ever have talked so. There is in the natural world a real movement, genuine happenings which never exactly repeat themselves, newness as well as continuity. Nature has a history. From primeval beginnings, so far as our present cosmic epoch is concerned, there has been change from inchoate motions of energy on to the appearance of ever more highly complicated or complex structures, themselves groupings or societies of energy-events, to living matter, to conscious beings, to man himself. This historical movement in the natural order has been outlined brilliantly and beautifully by Pierre Teilhard de Chardin in his *The Phenomenon of Man* and more briefly in a subsequent volume of essays called *Human Energy*.

Man in his historical existence is emergent from this natural world. He is not an alien intruder like an actor who walks upon a stage provided for him by nature but has no real part and place in that context. What goes on in the realm of human existence, with its eventful development which we call history, is indicative of the kind of on-going which takes place throughout the cosmos. I have said "the *kind* of on-going," for I do not wish to suggest that there is an exact and precise parallel between the historical and the natural. There are analogies, however, and these analogies must be taken with utmost seriousness. Thus a study of "lived" human experience, in its setting in a series of events, offers us an insight into the dynamics of the process as a whole. It indicates something of the way in which the process structures its dynamics so that they do not end in chaos or confusion but proceed in a fashion which, on the whole, is orderly and consistent, toward ends that may be achieved. The qualification "on the whole" is required since there are the "drags" and backward tendencies, the "diminishments" (in Teilhard's word), the setbacks, and the deviations which can and do impede the on-going creative advance. They do not succeed in stopping it because in a remarkable way the inexhaustible divine reality who is chief cause and final recipient of what occurs is able to use even these retrogressive factors to secure a continuation of the movement toward goals which are good and in which the various successive entities or energy-events may participate.

In a world like that, it is utterly incredible to talk as if history could be split from nature. Nature has a history, we have just said. We have also said that history has a geography. By this we mean that historical events have their situation in the world which includes the "lower" ranges of the creative process—the dust and dirt of things, the material world, the "round of the seasons," the climate, and much else. It is one of the merits of Arnold Toynbee's writing on history to have insisted again and again on the way in which these natural factors affect and influence what happens in human affairs, in human societies, and in the development of cultures. To cut history off from nature would be to commit what Whitehead styled "the fallacy of false bifurcation." Alas, a not inconsiderable number of theologians have fallen victim to this fallacy during the past half-century. They read the Scriptures through spectacles borrowed, albeit unconsciously, from certain varieties of idealist thought. The result has been a neglect of the strong emphasis in the Bible upon God's activity in the natural order, of which, perhaps, the obvious symbol is the "bow in the clouds" associated with God's "treaty of peace" with his human children after "the Flood." There are many other such symbols, however, to show that the Jewish mind would not be content to departmentalize the divine activity in creation. It was all of a piece; God worked in nature and he worked in the events of human experience; he also worked in such a way that each had its influence upon the other. Christianity, as the child of Judaism in so many ways, has followed the same line of thought, and of this we may note the sacramentalism of the Christian tradition as the outstanding example. Bread and wine and water, things of the natural order, are gladly used in Christian worship as a means whereby the historical situation of men is affected.

The mistaken attitude which would split nature from history was demonstrated in my own hearing some time ago by a distinguished scholar who was speaking of the essential elements in the Jewish tradition. He stated flatly that the Jews traditionally had never taught about "holy places" but only about "holy times"—his example was the Sabbath. He said that the Jew could not think of "holy places" because that would have been to reduce his faith to a matter concerned with nature, whereas that faith was essentially historical. But I could not help recalling that the Old Testament has much to say about the "holy land," the "holy city," and perhaps above all about the Temple and its sanctuary as the "holy place"—it was astonishing that this scholar had used, in a pejorative sense, the very phrase which for a Jew indicated the most sacred reality in his life, so sacred indeed that but once in the year could the high priest enter. Surely the Jews did not neglect "holy times" nor the history in which those times were set, but neither did they fail to recognize that these times had their given situation.

It so happened that the scholar in question had been much influenced by certain existentialist interpretations of religion in which very slight attention had been given to nature. Existentialist analysis of what it feels like to be human is of enormous value and I should be the first to welcome its insights; but one of its dangers has been precisely this lack of concern with the natural order. Yet a careful study of the Scriptures demonstrates the biblical wholeness of view; we need only to think of passages in the Psalter, references in Isaiah, and the association of Jahweh in primitive Judaism with volcanic eruptions, storms, and the like. The lecturer might have come to see that the existentialist stress on historical human experience, central as it is, must be supplemented by a wider cosmological reference if it is to be adequate both to what the Scriptures have to tell us and also to the concrete existence of men and women in every age.

The question before us is history in all its meanings, as these are related to the Christian faith which finds God specifically in his revelatory and redemptive action in Jesus of Nazareth. We are greatly in need of some balanced portrayal of the historical as it finds its place in that faith. This demands, among other things, that we understand history in its natural setting; it also requires that we see nature as providing more than a context for the realm of human events. Furthermore, we need to take into our picture the figure of Jesus as one who in fact lived in this world of happenings, so that he himself is an happening; while we need also to recognize how the community of which he is the origin and for which he is the foundation is itself ploughed into that realm of happening, where it continues its existence and through its members lives out its history.

Finally, we need to see how history is fulfilled in God. This will demand very careful consideration as we come to our final chapter. But one thing is quite clear: to speak of history as fulfilled in God does not mean the abrogation of history altogether at some "last time." Here again we can be much helped by process thought, since in that conceptuality God himself is seen as having a history and whatever we may intend when we speak of the divine "eternity" we cannot mean that God is "timeless." Maybe God's "eternity" is to be understood as eminent temporality in which all that historical happening of whatever type has accomplished and signified is taken and used for the abiding purposes which are his. So at least I believe; and believing it, I am prepared to say that the happenings in the world in process make a genuine and valuable contribution to the enrichment of the divine life, although God always remains unchangeably God in his faithfulness, integrity, relatedness to creation, and sacrificial and triumphant love.

CHAPTER 2

The Bible and History

Is the Bible a "history book?" And if it is not, to what type of literature does it belong?

These would have been questions which for the greater part of the long Christian tradition would not have been asked, at least in the sense in which we are now putting them. If not for our fathers, then certainly for our grandfathers, the Bible was "Holy Writ." It was entirely *sui generis,* not to be compared with any other writings. It was "the Word of God written," as one of the Articles of the Church of England puts it; hence it could not be categorized in the way in which one might assign other ancient books or collections of books to a specific literary genre. The fact that we today can ask such questions is an indication of the enormous change that has been wrought by scholarship during the past hundred years and a sign that the Bible is considered to be, in many if not in all respects, just like any other book.

Of course it was recognized in earlier days that the Bible contained a great variety of material. Nobody could have opened its pages and glanced through its contents without being aware of that. Further, it was well understood that different parts of the Bible required reading in special ways. From the day when Origen, typical of the Alexandrine school of Christian Platonists and himself a great biblical scholar, made distinctions in the biblical material between the literal and the mystical, with a mode of interpretation considered appropriate to the passages in question but with varieties of meaning possible for any given single text, the theologians of the Church have sought to "make sense of Scripture" by speaking of its levels of meaning. Two, three, four, even five different senses have been noted as possible; and there is a medieval jingle written to assist the student in distinguishing between them and thus knowing which type to use in a given instance. Nor was what we now know as biblical fundamentalism characteristic of the theologians of the ancient Church nor of the Reformation. That is a peculiarly modern, or near modern, phenomenon, which brings to the reading of Scripture the rationalistic presuppositions of the eighteenth century.

Nonetheless, this awareness on the part of the trained theologians did not seriously affect the way in which the ordinary Christian read his Bible. If he read it at all, in a day when literacy was not frequently found among such "ordinary" Christians, he read it as a holy book in which God spoke to men. That was that. Any and every part of it was equally inspired and hence equally the message of God to his human children. The Bible was revered in theory and often in practice; no other book could be considered worthy to be placed alongside it and often enough no object whatsoever could be put on top of it. The place which it was given in the ordinary pious home was supreme and unique.

Although Bible reading by lay people was not unknown before the Reformation, it was that revolutionary upheaval in the Church's existence which brought such reading to the forefront as a duty laid upon Christian people. The layman as well as the parson was not only free to read the Scriptures; he was admonished to do so, as the way in which his faith would be established and he would grow in his discipleship. Indeed, one of the reasons for teaching how to read was precisely to make possible this familiarity with Scripture. For many it was a great joy to be able to open the "holy book" and read whatever particular part happened to be before one. And since for most simple (and now literate) people, there was not sufficient knowledge of other literature to make comparisons possible, the Bible was simply taken as it stood. Its subtleties were either not noticed at all or were overlooked in the tremendous impact which the story of man's creation, fall, and redemption, found in Scripture, naturally made upon the one who read. Here was the source book of the Christian faith; even more, here was God's spoken message to men, "the Word of God inscripturated."

Neither Luther nor Calvin had much patience with the subtle distinctions made in the Middle Ages by the schoolmen in regard to the various levels or senses of Scripture. On the whole, they preferred what they took to be the straightforward (we might say the plain historical and literal) meaning of the words which they read. Obviously they were obliged to allow for something more than that sense alone. After all, parables were parables and not reporting of factual incidents; the Psalms, obviously, were hymns of praise or laments over evils and suffering and not statements whose patent significance could be assumed without enquiry. Yet the tendency of the great reformers was to distrust what they regarded with some justification as the excessive subtlty of scholastic theology; they sought to find a more direct and immediate meaning, plainly to be seen, and not requiring the careful discriminations and minute examination of every passage for its variety of possible significance according to the historical, moral, mystical, or theological intention of the written words.

None of the great reformers, we have said, can be called a fundamentalist in the modern sense of the word. They may have thought of the Bible as being what we have styled, following a contemporary conservative theologian, "the Word of God inscripturated"; they may have believed that it was all inspired by God in exactly the same way and must all be read in pretty much the same fashion. But they applied their own criteria to the study of Scripture. Luther insisted that it must be read in order to see how it pointed toward or drew men to Christ. He could reject the Epistle of St. James because he thought that it sought to reinstate a doctrine of justification by works rather than by faith: it was "an epistle of straw." Calvin was more intent on some literal meaning of the text; yet when one follows his exposition and interpretation of the various books of the Bible in his little-read commentaries, one can see that he was not unaware of the need for some care in getting at what the words of Scripture have to say. He did not treat the Bible as if it had simply dropped down from heaven; in his own way he was conscious of the setting of its several parts in a specific context and he tried to take this into account as he discussed the material. Yet despite the relative freedom which Luther, certainly, and also Calvin, to some degree, were prepared to use in the study of what both took to be the final authority for Christian faith, the fact that they centered attention on it and could read it without due regard for its (to us) inescapable setting in the living tradition of Christian faith, worship, and life, prepared the way for their followers—the scholastics of the Reformed churches—to look at the Bible in what seems almost a superstitious way.

Anybody today who reads the Bible, unless he belongs to a narrowly fundamentalist group, is almost certain to look at the book in a very different way. To him, the questions which we asked at the beginning come naturally, indeed inescapably. What sort of literature is the Bible? Is it a book of history in the conventional meaning given that phrase or is it something else?

In working toward answers to such questions, highly relevant to our present topic, there are some preliminary considerations which should be noted and discussed. First, the Bible is indeed "literature." It is not a single book but a collection of writings which are by no means to be taken as a whole—although there is a sense in which the Bible *is* a whole, to which we shall refer at a later point. That wholeness, however, is not found in its contents as superficially as they appear to the ordinary reader of printed volumes. The Bible, then, is what is now known as an anthology, in which there have been brought together a remarkable number of different pieces of writing, coming from different times and written with different intentions.

The second preliminary consideration is that the Bible, whatever else it may be, is the book of a community. It is "the

Church's book" and must be recognized and read as such. When I was young it was customary to say, in the Christian circles familiar to me, that "the Bible is to prove, the Church to teach." Certainly this was not a very happy way of making the point, as we shall see; yet there was a point to be made. The Christian community has its living faith in Jesus Christ which it must proclaim; it has its way of worship, and it has its life of obedience to God made known savingly in Christ. These have been articulated into beliefs which have been given theological formulation, worship according to a certain style (sometimes formalized, like the Eucharist), and the more or less precise codes of Christian conduct. These do not stand alone, as if they had been created without regard for the originating events from which the community takes its rise. They have their ground in and they find their validation through an appeal to that of which the Bible speaks. To cite once again a phrase from the Articles of Religion drawn up for the Church of England, the Church cannot require for faith leading to salvation anything that cannot be "proved by most certain warrants of Holy Scripture." When we recall that "proved" meant at that time "tested," we can see that what is being said is that developing Christian belief is always subject to examination in the light of the scriptural evidence—and the same can be said of developing modes of Christian worship and of the working out of the moral implications of Christian faith.

Yet this appeal is not made to an external and extraneous authority, as if the Bible were not integral to the community's on-going life. On the contrary, the Bible is in the peculiar position of being both an element (the central one) in the continuing life of the Christian Church and also the normative point in that tradition. Even the Roman Catholic Church, which at one time seemed to set up two authorities side-by-side, has now come to think differently. At Vatican II, the way in which Bible and Church tradition were related is not all that unlike the view of Reformed Christians. On the other hand, the latter Christian groups have come more and more to recognize the place of tradition in the Christian enterprise and to seek to restore the Bible to its place within the developing life of the Church. They too wish to speak of the Bible as "the Church's book," although they insist vigorously on its authoritative quality as determinative of whether or not the living tradition is true to its essential spirit or nature.

These two considerations—that the Bible is an anthology, from the literary point of view, and that it is the authoritative book of a living Christian community—help us to see how we are to approach the reading of the Scriptures, both for theological purposes and for the deepening of the Christian's life in grace. But they do not provide an answer to the questions with which we began this chapter. It is to those questions we now turn, remembering the anthological character of the Bible and its nature as produced within a community of faith which yet regards it with special reverence as being in some genuine sense a norm to which appeal must be made.

If the Bible is a collection or anthology of writings, it is also a collection of writings of most various types. It has to do with history in the obvious sense of the word—that is, it talks about events or what were believed to have been events. Thus it is, to some degree anyway, a "history book." But that is too simple a way of phrasing the fact. The books which are included in the Bible and which recount incidents remembered and told in Jewish circles—such as how the people got into the Holy Land and their adventures on the way, the early days of settlement and conflict with the native Canaanites, the "court chronicle" of David (where we seem to touch what to us is "real" historical narrative), and the like—have to do with what was taken to be factual occurrences. Yet the way of telling is not that of straightforward historical narrative, such as modern writers have often used; the whole material, even in the "court chronicle," is given with an edificatory intention—it is to build up the faith of those who would first hear the stories and later those who would read them once they were put down in writing.

But if the Bible has to do with history, in some of its parts, it contains a great deal of other material. There is much Jewish poetry, of which the Psalms will serve as an example, while in the prophetic writings (Isaiah particularly, whether we are thinking of the earlier prophet or of the later "Second Isaiah" of the latter part of the book called by that name) there is also much poetical material. There are stories in the modern sense of invented narratives to illustrate or teach an important religious or moral truth; here the Book of Jonah will serve as the best instance—and one can only wonder at the unimaginative people who for so long, in the Christian tradition, regarded this as an account of an actual incident, with the problem then arising of Jonah and the whale. There are love lyrics, in particular the beautiful Song of Songs, which originally did not have a specifically religious purpose but was a remembered composition expressing the passionate relationship of two Jewish lovers. There are "secular" tales like that of Esther, where the word "God" is not mentioned but in which there is a desire to show racial loyalty on the part of Jews when they were forced to submit to foreign domination.

Anthologies of "wise sayings," such as Proverbs and Ecclesiastes, are also included. There is the profoundly tragic, yet deeply moving, story of Job and his sufferings, dealing with the problem of unmerited suffering. This is no historical account but a magnificent poetical attempt to treat an issue which greatly troubled those who had come to believe that the good man would have his sufficient "reward" in this life. The concept of a "future life" was hardly a prominent feature of Judaism, if it was held at all. The departed were in Sheol, a dim and ghostly place where spirits continued without hope or meaning, but this was hardly a belief that promised much to those who were forced to suffer here and now, especially those who had been faithful to Jahweh and had no reason to feel that they would be compelled to experience the dereliction portrayed as happening to Job.

There are also the various books with apocalyptic intention, telling in figurative language about "the end," with the purpose of making God's will plain in the present moment. These were later compositions, coming from Judaism's times of trouble; they are messages of reassurance, cast often in narrative form (Daniel is the best instance here) telling of fictitious past events or future occurrences, but with specific reference to the contemporary situation. Finally there is the prophetic material, sometimes actually written by the prophet himself and sometimes a recalling of spoken oracles which a follower or a school of followers have set down. The prophetic material, despite a popular misunderstanding, is not concerned so much to foretell future events—although this does enter the picture—as to announce vividly and clearly God's judgment on, his will for, and his intentions in respect to, the "chosen people" and by extension the world at large. In a way, this prophetic material is the most striking in the Old Testament, for here we have to do with words spoken by men whose insight into the reality of the God-man relationship, the purpose of God in the course of nature and history, and the future accomplishment of the divine will, as well as the depth of human motivation and desire, is unparalleled in any other literature.

So far, we have been speaking of the Old Testament. When we turn to the New Testament we find a similar variety of material, although not the wide range present in the Old. The gospels are collections of oral traditions told about Jesus and handed down within the primitive Christian community. This is plain enough in respect to the gospels of Matthew, Mark, and Luke; it is also true of John, or the fourth gospel. In each case, the material has to do with what were taken to be actual occurrences in a period very shortly before the setting down of the traditions. But the purpose with which the collections were made, like the purpose of the original oral use, was not historical in the chronological or strictly factual sense. The majority of New Testament scholars agree that the telling about what Jesus was believed to have said and done, as well as what happened to him, is always in terms of who he is now accepted as being. Jesus is the risen Lord, the one in whom

28

the primitive community rested its faith; since he is just this, what "he began both to do and to teach," to use Luke's words from Acts, has its great importance. Doubtless, the belief in Jesus has affected the things told about him. Hence, we are not confronted by strictly biographical data, such as we today might have expected; we have a theological determination of what is told about the central figure and his teaching and actions. We have already commented on this point in Chapter 1.

The epistles form still another type of New Testament material. Some of them are versions of what appear actually to have been what the word suggests: letters written by Christian leaders to Christian churches or to particular persons. Some of them are more like theological treatises cast in epistolary form. Romans is a good example of the latter. The so-called Epistle to the Hebrews, by an unknown early Christian thinker, is another. Such documents are explorations of problems which would naturally arise under the historical circumstances of the first Christian community—the relationship of Christian faith to older Judaism, the significance of Jesus as Savior, the meaning of the new life found in him, the significance of redemption such as Christians believed had been given through his death and resurrection, and many others. Similarly in the epistles, which are actually letters, there is discussion of problems, as for example in I Corinthians where St. Paul deals with issues that have arisen in the Corinthian Christian Church and seeks to provide helpful answers to questions which evidently they have asked.

The Acts of the Apostles, doubtless by the writer of the second gospel or Luke, purports to be an account of the early days of the Christian fellowship as it spread from Palestine through the Greco-Roman world under St. Peter and then under St. Paul. The story takes us up to the time when finally St. Paul arrived at the imperial city of Rome. There is no doubt a good deal of factual reporting in this book, such as the obviously first-hand section about the last of Paul's journeys which took him to Rome after his appeal to Caesar when arrested in

Jerusalem. This has been called a "travel diary," so much verisimilitude seems to be found in its account. Yet the whole of Acts, however much of its contents may have a factual basis, is told with a theological interest. If the gospels have to do with what Jesus "began to do and to teach," Acts has to do with what, through the Spirit, he continued to do and teach in and through those who were committed to him and who proclaimed his saving significance to Gentiles in many parts of the Mediterranean world.

Finally, we have the strange document called the Revelation of St. John the Divine, a Christian equivalent of Jewish apocalyptic writing. Here some author has managed to combine material taken from Jewish apocalyptic sources with specifically Christian visions having to do with the lordship and sovereignty of the risen Christ. The Jewish material has been edited in such a way that it can be read in a Christian sense. It was highly relevant to, and doubtless great encouragement for, members of Christian groups who were facing the dangers of persecution during the latter part of the first century or the early years of the second.

In the last few paragraphs we have given a very rough summary of the types of material contained in the collection known as the Bible. We need to remember that the collection as we have it did not come into existence in some once-for-all fashion. The Jewish community gradually accepted the writings found in the Old Testament and at the Council of Jamnia, in the Christian era, gave them a sort of quasi-canonical status. The New Testament books were not accepted in their present form for quite a considerable period. Indeed it was not until the third century, and in some respects even slightly later, that a definite limit was set for admission to the canon. And even in our own time there is a difference between the version of the Bible used in the Roman Catholic Church, which includes the intertestamentary literature known as the Apocrypha, and the version used in Reformed churches, which does not accept this material as part of the Scriptures. Anglicans, true to their mediating position, take the

30

Apocrypha as worthy of attention for edification but not for doctrinal purposes.

The purpose of this long treatment of the types of biblical material has been to show that it is inaccurate to speak of the Bible as a whole as primarily an "historical book." The Bible includes historical material in that it contains the reports familiar to Jews and Christians about events in the past. But it includes a great deal more, while even that historical data is presented in a way which is very different from that taken by modern "scientific" history and even from that taken by earlier historians whose primary interest has been in chronology and annal. Certainly chronology and annal are present in the Old Testament—lists of kings show this—but even then the main significance is elsewhere. Lists such as these are given to show the continuity of the life of the Jewish people, in times of prosperity and of adversity, rather than to provide later generations with data that is supposed to be "objectively" important. Thus we are now led to consider the question of the Bible and history. How does the Bible see history?

Phrased like that, the question can be misleading, for there is no such thing as "the Bible"; there are diversities of viewpoints within a grand and comprehensive unity of faith. Yet we can speak intelligibly about the main line of development and we can certainly say that, for the most part, the material found in Scripture has a conception of the realm of events which was characteristic of the Jewish mind and was continued into the Christian era.

How does the Bible, in the large sense just noted, appear to regard the past, present, and future series of events—that is, how does it deal with the "historical" material which it contains and the way in which the other "non-historical" material is affected by this manner of treatment?

The first point to be made is that the biblical writers do not appear to have been much interested in history as such, if by this we intend the account of the past simply for its own sake. This statement needs some qualification, perhaps, since it may be the case that the court chronicle of King David was written more or less with this intention; yet on the whole and in the main the interest of the biblical writers is elsewhere. What is that interest?

Put very briefly, we may say that it is in what the past, remembered and handed down, has to say about the present and future. That is, the events which preceded the spoken or written word were taken to illuminate and make sense of the experience of the Jewish people for whom the material was made available. An historical sense, in the meaning which we should give that phrase, is a fairly recent acquisition for men. Not that they were not concerned about what had taken place before their time, of course, but that the reason for their concern and the use they made of what they knew of earlier happening was primarily in giving the significance of what, at the present moment, they believed or did. We can see an excellent example in the way in which the Jewish Passover Meal is held, even today. Of course the meal looks back, as we would say, to the supposed deliverance of the Jews from the Egyptians, when they "passed over" the Sea of Reeds, fortified only by a hastily prepared meal. But when the question is asked, "What mean ye by this service?" the Jew would not reply that he intends historical reminiscence, as if the meal were a rite in which something that occurred long ago was commemorated and nothing more was signified. On the contrary, the meaning of the Passover Meal is the present relationship of the Jewish people with the God who in the past delivered them from their enemies, who during their long history has been their ruler and guide, and who at this very moment is the God of Abraham and Isaac and Jacob—and of Moses leading their ancestors to freedom. Because God had done in the past what the story of the Passover relates, he is accepted in the present as the sovereign Lord and he is confidently believed to promise for his people a future which will be for their good and for his glory. "Next year, in Jerusalem," the Jews used to say—not now, for they were still exiled from their "homeland," but in God's good time ("next year") they would be able to eat the Passover in the place which to them was sacred because God had given it to them as their very own home.

When an ancient Jewish writer gathered the myths about creation and moulded them into a continuous narrative—whether in the more formal shape of the first creation story in Genesis or the more naive story which follows—he was not engaging in what those who read would regard as a blow-by-blow description of how the world came into existence, under the hand of God and through the exercise of divine power. His purpose in telling of creation was to stress the continual dependence of all men, but especially of the Jews who knew God with special intimacy, upon the hand and the power of that creative deity. When another Jewish writer told of the wanderings of the patriarchs until their initial settlement in the Holy Land, his intention was not so much to report ascertained or ascertainable facts, although doubtless he believed that the stories were "true," as it was to show that God's guidance was with his chosen people, in the past to bring them into the land of Canaan and in the present to be with them in all their struggles, joys, and sorrows. They were in the land that God had given them; he meant it to be kept holy to him by those who knew and accepted their calling to be his caretakers or stewards.

Or again, when the long saga of the exodus from Egypt and the entrance into Canaan was told, with the years of wandering in the wilderness, the point of the narrative, in both forms in which we find it (J and E material, as the critics say), is to show that the people of Israel were and still are God's "chosen," whom he has taken to himself and made his own, whom he has led through trouble and struggle, to whom he has shown loving favor, and from whom he requires utter obedience to his will and the fulfillment of the covenant which he had made with their fathers. What God has done in the past is a demonstration of what he is in the present; and both are assurance that he will be faithful in the future. And if this is true, then the requirement which is made of his people here and now is the loyalty which will be both pleasing to God and fulfilling of their own destiny as his faithful servants.

Much the same can be said about the New Testament books. While there are many indubitable factual elements in the gospel narratives, for example, the editors of those books were not primarily interested in writing something like Caesar's *Gallic Wars,* to take an ancient instance, or like some modern biography of Winston Churchill or Mahatma Gandhi. Their first concern was to convey to the Christian community, of which they were members, a series of stories, found in the continuing teaching of the Church, which would clearly bring out the significance of Jesus Christ as shown in the events which were central to the Christian experience. Thus, Mark's gospel opens with the words, "The beginning of the gospel of Jesus Christ the Son of God." What do these words mean? Certainly not "beginning" only in the sense of reported events or remembered incidents although that has its place in the whole complex. What is intended is "beginning" in the sense of a telling of the total event-response which produced the conviction that an historical figure named Jesus, now taken by the Christian fellowship to be God's Messiah or Christ, is in a very special sense God's Son; and at the very moment when the material is being set down, that Christ is the active, living, present Lord who is to be accepted as such and to whom the evangelist's fellow believers commit themselves in faith without reserve or hesitation.

In similar fashion, the compiler or writer of the fourth gospel tells his readers that while there is a great deal of remembered material concerning Jesus—so much, indeed, that "the whole world could not contain the books" which might be written to tell it—yet what *is* included by him in his gospel is placed there with the explicit purpose which he states: "That ye may believe that Jesus is the Christ, the Son of God, and that believing ye may have life in his name." Incidently, the reference to the number of books that might be written has its point, too; for surely the writer intends to include here what has happened in consequence of Jesus' coming as well as what happened in that coming. This is another way, perhaps, of making the same, or a similar, theological assertion about the significance of the One concerning whom the narratives are told. And even though the reference to the number of books that might be written is from the twenty-first chapter of the gospel, which most critics suppose to be an appendix to the original draft, while the latter reference (to the purpose of writing) is from the twentieth chapter, ending what is thought to be the original draft, the point I am making is not affected. Whoever wrote what and when, the gospel as it stands and as it is accepted and used within the Christian Church, is in integral whole. The two verses can be read together, as signifying something important for the Christians who first read them, even if they are separated by some twenty-four verses and may have come from different writers.

The opening words of the Acts of the Apostles are another indication of the point here being made. The author writes to Theophilus, who may or may not have been a genuine personage (the name means "God-lover"), that in his first book, presumably the gospel according to St. Luke, he had dealt with what Jesus "began to do and to teach." Now he is undertaking to tell of what had happened after Jesus "had been taken up," but before that event had "presented himself alive to the apostles" as a prelude to that ascension. This, as we have seen, is evidently intended to be what Jesus continued (and was still continuing as the book was written) to do and to teach. Why is the author making this effort? For two reasons, it seems. First, he wants to show that the Christian gospel and the community which carries it are legitimate heirs of the ancient Jewish faith; hence the Christian churches were legally permissible in the Roman Empire, which had granted Judaism the status of a *religio licita* which could be practiced without contravening Roman requirements. And second, and much more important, was the writer's wish to awaken contemporary Christian believers to the situation in which they themselves were placed. They were not only heirs of the promises

35

made by God in the older dispensation; they were also members of the community of faith now reconstituted by God on the foundation of Jesus Christ as his Son and Christ and hence recipients of the Holy Spirit released in and through the event of Jesus Christ to make that community "Israel after the Spirit." Nor was this all. They had become heirs of all that God purposed for his children because they had heard and accepted the message of salvation in Christ. Nor was this only in the past. At the present moment they were still hearing that Word, still responding to it, still recipients of the Spirit. That was what their Christian profession was all about. And if this was the case, then the demand was laid upon them to follow the great figures of Acts, first Peter and then Paul, in utter obedience to God known in Christ. In doing this, they were to be like Paul who in Rome "welcomed all who came to him, preaching the Kingdom of God and teaching about the Lord Jesus Christ."

What the writers of the New Testament are interested in doing, as an obligation laid upon them as faithful disciples of the Lord, is to show that because of what God was remembered to have done in the past, he could be trusted to act consistently with his purpose in the future, while enormous requirements were laid on his newly "chosen people" in the present. Furthermore, because of what God had done in the past and chiefly in the sending of his Son, he was to be known as the God whom his people could and would and did encounter, in whom they could utterly trust, and to whose loyal service it was their privilege to give themselves soul and body.

In sum, then, it must be said that the biblical material as a whole, and in its main line of teaching, can only rightly be understood when it is seen as intended to open a present or contemporary relationship with God, invoked and enabled by what this same God has disclosed himself as doing, and hence as being, in the events to which the community looks as its origin and its providentially guided continuation. Because God has done these things, because he is confidently to be trusted in the contemporary situation, he is also to be accepted as the Lord of the future. He is able and willing, as he is also consistently active, to fulfill in that future what even now he has shown himself as purposing for his children and for the world.

Thus we are brought back to the point made in our second preliminary consideration earlier in this chapter. The Bible cannot rightly be interpreted unless it is seen as the book of the Church, whether this means the Old Testament as the book of the people of Israel or the whole of Scripture, Old and New Testaments, as the book of the Christian community. A failure to grasp this is bound to result in a misreading of the Bible. It will be treated either as an interesting collection of religious literature only, or it will be taken as in its literal sense the unmediated word of God to his children, or it will be read mechanically and without regard for the context in which every part of it had its origin and which alone can provide its proper significance.

To see the Bible in this way is not easy for those who have been brought up in the older but mistaken conception of its significance. For such people it often appears that this approach imperils the central place which rightly they feel the Bible must have in their discipleship, while at the same time it may seem to reduce what it does have to tell them to the relativity of the Christian community's beliefs and practice at a given moment of time or in some particular situation. But these fears are quite groundless. Through no fault of their own but because of erroneous teaching (however well-intentioned) they are attempting to read and to use the Scriptures in a fashion in which the Christian Church, in its main stream of tradition, has always refused to read and use it. In that main stream, the Scriptures have unfailingly been put in the context of the Church's contemporary existence. To lose sight of this context is to pin one's faith on something other than the living God of this present moment, about whom the Bible speaks so compellingly and clearly.

We have seen how the biblical material itself looks at the events in the past about which it tells. We must now show how the Christian Church has used the Bible in a fashion which is consonant with this attitude. I believe that our best clue here is provided when we turn to the lections which are officially appointed to be read in the course of the celebration of the Eucharist—at least in certain churches, Catholic, Orthodox, Anglican, Lutheran among them—and attempt to understand their place in that central moment of Christian worship. We shall then look at the way in which the theologians of the Patristic Age and later referred to the Scriptures as they went about their work of thinking through the meaning of what those Scriptures had to tell them.

I have just opened the Book of Common Prayer, at random. The page which is before me contains the collect, epistle and gospel for the Third Sunday after Trinity. The collect is a prayer that God's people, to whom he has given "an hearty desire to pray," may by his help "be defended and comforted in all dangers and adversities." This collect sets the special theme for the Sunday; if I had chanced to open the Prayer Book to Christmas or Good Friday or Easter Day or to some saint's or holy day, this setting of a theme would have been even more obviously in accordance with the special significance which has been attached to such a day in the Church's year. The appointed epistle is I Peter 5:5ff., which is an admonition to early Christians to "humble themselves" before God, to "cast their care" on him, to see that while "the devil, as a roaring lion, walketh about seeking whom he may devour," God as disclosed in Jesus Christ will yet "stablish, strengthen, settle" those who in faith commit themselves to him. The appointed gospel for III Trinity is Luke 15:1ff.—the teaching of Jesus about the lost sheep, the lost coin, and the "joy in the presence of the angels of God over one sinner that repenteth." In other words, the gospel is a proclamation of God's seeking and finding those who are alienated from him, who are lost, and who are lonely without his presence and his gracious action realized in their hearts as constant toward them.

I believe that any worshipper at the Holy Communion on the

Third Sunday after Trinity, hearing the collect, epistle, and gospel read by the officiating minister, will grasp with no difficulty (provided he attends to what he hears) what these have to tell him. The collect of course is addressed to God but it "collects" those who are present and their needs and desires in a single appeal for help in "dangers and adversities." The epistle sets forth the attitude proper to the Christian in all times and places, but more especially when he must face temptation, inner evils, or external difficulties pressing in upon him on certain occasions. Originally concerned with Christians in a very early period of the Church, it is lifted out of but not removed entirely from that context in the past so that it becomes meaningful to the worshipper in his own immediate situation. The gospel, reporting remembered teaching of Jesus, has a significance much more compelling than recollection of words presumably spoken in the far-distant past. It provides the assurance, through those words, that because God has disclosed himself as sovereign love in Jesus Christ, he can be trusted never to leave his children helpless and alone, never desert them in trouble, never fail to seek for them wherever they may have wandered, never give them up no matter how disobedient to him they may have been. They may feel themselves lonely, distant from his felt or experienced presence, neglected or uncared for; nonetheless, God is there, seeking them, loving them, yearning to bring them to himself if only they will hear his voice as he calls them.

My point ought to be obvious. The two sections, taken as I have said at random, are an indication of how the Christian Church in its main tradition has read and used the Bible. It has not been overly concerned about the details of fact which in the distant past may or may not have occurred precisely as reported; it has not looked at the Scriptures as presenting us with a "problem" that must be solved, as to how much or in what way this reportage is accurate in its remembrance. It has trusted that the Scriptures do tell us of what God accomplished in the events of the past, through his "mighty acts" in the realm of happening;

39

but it has taken the passages which tell of such happenings, as well as everything else in Scripture that has been chosen for use, as a way in which now, here, in the present moment where the believer stands, God's character, his action, his redemptive love, his forgiveness and acceptance of his children are disclosed. In the Scriptures of the Old and New Testament, taken together and grasped in the wholeness of their message, God still speaks to his children—not in separation from their brethren but precisely in their social belonging to the community where he is adored and obeyed.

This does not mean that the Church has used Scripture as if it were what publishers and book reviewers sometimes describe as "an inspirational book," designed to provide for those who read or hear it some exalted sentiments. Insofar as the Bible is read privately by the believer, it may indeed "inspire him," although in a very different sense from the one I have just caricatured. Its inspiration will be exactly like that noted of the public use of Scripture. It will build him up in the faith and it will assure him through what it says about the past (in its variety of ways) and through its other types of writing that God remains and for ever will be his "refuge and strength, a very present help in times of trouble." It will proclaim this same God as cosmic lover of his world and of men. By speaking of what God has done, it will enable him to see more clearly what God must be doing even now; it will give him courage to believe that for the future, God may be trusted to be what in the past and present he has revealed himself as being.

In other words, both in the liturgical use of Scripture and in the private reading of it, the present reality of God's love-in-action in his world and for his children, is brought directly and immediately to bear upon this man, this congregation of believers, this age of the Christian Church. Using the Bible so, we are in agreement with the way the total collection itself looks at history—the past is brought into the present, and both illuminate the future.

We now turn to a very brief summary of the way in which Scripture had its place in the theological constructions of the Patristic Age and a glance at its use for the same purpose in some of the later work of theologians. First, it is to be noted that despite an appearance to the contrary, the Bible was not used as a mine from which proof texts might be extracted. This may seem to be the case because of the odd bits of Scripture which are sometimes found cited in such theological efforts. But the approach was really quite different. The faith in its wholeness was understood, so far as may be, by early theologians through their participation in the life of the Church. Here they found both edification and inspiration (in the sense in which we have used the latter word). For example, St. Athanasius constantly refers to the life in grace, empowering and enabling men; any doctrine which would threaten or damage that known life is to be rejected. Scripture has its place in this setting, since the biblical material both provides the necessary originating source of the new life and also validates its reality by speaking directly as from God to the believing community. The Scriptural writings were used to back up, to confirm, and to safeguard the faith which made possible the life in grace.

We have observed the various levels of interpretation used by early theologians. They employed these levels in order to get at what they were sure must be the proper sense of the biblical texts, in the light of the specific purposes which they had in view as they worked out a statement of the faith. The Scriptures were normative, but in their literal sense they were not supposed to be infallible utterances; the very variety of levels of meaning guarded against that error. St. Augustine had as high a view of Scripture as any ancient theologian; yet it was he who said that "the Scriptures are to be believed only on the authority of the Church." He did not mean simply that the Church had given them a position which was supreme, but also that it was the abiding faith in God in Christ, held by the Church, which made it possible to use the Bible as an illuminating document which must

41

be consulted before any formulation could be accepted as correct. The total biblical witness to God and his character, the divine purpose for the world and for men, the position of humans as God's children yet in sin and requiring redemption, the destiny of the world and of man, and all the rest, was never taken in isolation from this living faith which the community held and which it proclaimed.

Luther and Calvin, not to mention Thomas Aquinas before them, were equally building upon the faith which the community proclaimed and taught. The former were more intent on literal interpretation than Aquinas, but as we have seen they were not fundamentalists in the modern sense. Only when some of the successors of these Reformers and some of the literal-minded theologians of the post-Tridentine Roman Church appeared was theological labor restricted to an explication of the actual words of the Bible in their obvious "seen-at-a-glance" significance. And in putting it in this way we have been unfair to those theologians who wrestled long and hard to make the words of Scripture agree with what already they believed because the general consensus of Christian faith taught it; while in the Roman Church the dubious addition of "tradition" as "along-side" Scripture averted the worst mistakes. Yet one must allow that this notion of "tradition," wrongly stated in the period in question, was at least correct in refusing to put the Scriptures in an isolated and omnicompetent place for theological purposes. Happily, the new way of seeing tradition, in the Roman Church, and the openness to the continuity of the living faith, in the Reformed churches, are helping us to come to a sounder appreciation of the way Bible and abiding Christian witness in community are related.

The rise of biblical criticism has delivered us from many errors, even if it has also raised for us many problems of which our ancestors were unaware. There are still some theologians, however, who accept in word the new perspective which this critical approach has made possible, but in their actual job of theologizing unfortunately tend to forget what they have accepted. Then we have the kind of "biblical theology" which assumes that by an arrangement of presumed scriptural motifs or by the systematizing of biblical images or "types," or in some other way, it is possible to use the Scriptures alone for the construction of a sound theology. On the other hand, biblical theologians like Karl Barth do not fall victim to any such fallacy. An examination of Barth's conscientious but very selective use of Scripture, in respect (to give one example) of the doctrine of predestination, is highly instructive. He balances and weighs the various pieces of biblical material in the light of convictions which in the last resort (and not always with adequate acknowledgement) he has drawn from the faith of the living Christian community and its assured life in grace.

All this brings us back finally to the point urged some pages before. Christian faith is pinned to the living God of whom the Bible speaks, rather than to the Bible which speaks about him. How then does history enter the picture? It enters because it is in terms of the remembered past, treasured in the Church's living memory and set down in divers forms in the Scriptures, that the character and faithfulness of God, his love, his consistency in action in all times and places, are vividly and compellingly brought to the attention of those who are members of the fellowship which those events brought into existence. The past is known in terms of the response which has been made to it; it does not stand abstractly and in separation from such response. The historical aspect of the biblical literature is of supreme significance to us because it is never a dead past, something which took place a long time ago and which is now, to all intents and purposes, simply a matter of ancient chronicle. It is a living and present past.

CHAPTER 3

The Meaning of History Today

One of the difficulties with language, and not least with the English language, is that there are not always words which will show subtle distinctions or nuances of meaning within some general sense of a given idea. Often we wish to be able to give some special shading to an idea and we find it next to impossible to do this with the words actually at our disposal.

It has often been remarked that the vocable "word" is itself unsatisfactory in just this respect. We can say "word" when we intend merely a vocable; hence, we use "words" when we talk and they mean certain sounds made by our mouths and heard by the ears of other people. But we can also want to talk about some message which we have received; here too we often use "word" to describe it, as when we say "I had word from him the other day." Or we can wish to speak about the expression of an idea in our minds, in such a way that others will be enabled to grasp that idea through the speech which we must use if we are to communicate; here too "word" is the vocable which we employ. And a Christian theologian has to deal with the Greek term *Logos*, commonly translated "Word" (with the capital letter), as the term which traditionally has pointed to God in his out-going, self-revealing, and truth-disclosing *hypostasis,* the second person of the Triune Deity. Here the use of the term "Word" is validated for us by its long use in theological discussion and writing. Yet the translation in that way of the Greek *Logos* does not quite manage to convey the many associations which the original word had in the time when first it was used—associations which have to do with a variety of Jewish ideas about God's "Wisdom," his "Truth," his "Act," and the like, as well as specifically Hellenistic ideas such as are found in the writings of the Hellenistic Jewish philosopher Philo and also in a number of pagan thinkers who employed the same term to denote the rationality of the cosmos, the truth of the nature of things, and several other ideas.

Other languages may be in a better case now and again. In Latin, for example, it is possible to speak of *vox,* or *sermo,* or *verbum,* depending upon what we wish to convey. But there is also *ratio*; and possibly other terms might be cited. In French we can distinguish between *mot* and *verbe,* to name but two possibilities. Greek gives us, among others, *rhema* and *logos.* Yet even in those languages, we are not without difficulties when we want to make subtle distinctions and at the same time indicate some common area with which the term chosen has to do.

The word "history" is a striking instance of this difficulty. So far in this book I have always tried to be clear about the particular sense which was intended whenever the word "history" (or its adjective, "historical") has been employed. The context too may have helped the reader to determine in just what way I have meant the word. Yet I do not doubt that there have been places where my use of "history" may have caused some confusion, not only because of unconscious carelessness on my own part but also because there are such shades of meaning in "history" that the reader himself, bringing to this book his own attitudes and ideas, may have failed to see the precise significance of a particular use of the term. As I remarked earlier, this was illustrated for me some years ago when in a seminar I was conducting, with some fifteen research students in attendance, I noted down some thirteen different ways in which they had used "history" and "historical." They were discussing with me the history of Christian doctrine; the specific topic for the day was "Christianity's Historical Basis as Understood in the Early Church." And at the end of the two hours, I had the sad feeling that we had been talking much of the time at cross-purposes.

Each of the young men who had contributed had brought his own nuance of "history"; each who listened had thought in his own special way. The result of it all was a decision to give another two hours to a discussion of the very word itself—but I must confess that we did not get much enlightenment when we had finished.

The reader may be relieved to know that I do not intend to discuss thirteen possible meanings of "history" in the present chapter, but I do wish to look at several senses in which, in our own day, the word has been and is being used. The first thing to say is that there is in German a most helpful distinction, permitted fortunately by that language, between two ways of thinking about history—ways which can often be confused and consequently lead to considerable misunderstanding by those who are interested in how and why Christians should bother with history at all. In the first chapter I alluded to this distinction and mentioned the words, which are of course *historie* and *geschichte.*

To be sure, even Germans in ordinary speech can and do use these two words more or less interchangeably or shift from one to the other without being conscious of suggesting a different idea. Thus Rudolf Bultmann, whose main interest in this respect is to stress the *geschichte* aspect and put the *historie* aspect in a less important place, on at least some occasions—unless my memory fails me completely—uses one term where logically and consistently he should have used the other. But this quite human and perhaps inescapable failing apart, the distinction in the words' meaning is very helpful, although in my judgment it can be pressed so far that it may become almost absurd.

Generally speaking, *historie* signifies the sort of narrative or chronological reporting which may be written after a careful scientific enquiry into the "remains" of the past. Documents, state papers, diaries, and a host of other materials may be studied. As a result of such work, an historical account may be written which purports to be, at least in principle, an accurate record which is validated by extant and reliable evidence—which may

47

include, of course, archaeological remains and other kinds of evidence in addition to the written documents. Thus it is possible to establish 1066 as the date of the Norman Conquest of England. Americans can confidently assert that the Declaration of Independence was signed in the city of Philadelphia by a group of men whose names are known, at a date which documents indicate, and perhaps (although I am not sure of this) at a particular hour on that day.

When we come to ancient events, the *historie* is likely to be much less cartain; there is always a doubt about the exactitude of the references, the chance that some error has crept into the documentation, or the possibility that the ruins which have been excavated and explored may not have been interpreted in the right way. Yet few historical scholars would question the comparative accuracy of Caesar's crossing the Rubicon, his conquest of all Gaul in a given period of years, his assassination by a conspiracy of fellow Romans, and the coming to power of his adopted son who took to himself a series of titles to establish his authority and who became in the end the first "emperor" of Rome. The matter becomes much more complicated and difficult when the scholar must depend upon the probable value of old legends—say about Babylonia or some other ancient country—and other materials where it is very much a matter of probability of a high or low order. Yet it is commonly regarded as possible to say something fairly reliable about the *historie* of these ancient empires.

If this is the meaning of *historie*, the meaning of *geschichte* is quite distinct. Here what is intended is the significance of events or happenings as they have come to be interpreted in terms of some supposed value or purpose or meaning for those who doubtless believed that something did in fact take place in the *historie* sense. Thus what in one way is *historie* may in another way be *geschichte*, precisely because it has been interpreted and found to have some value or importance more profound than the mere fact that it did take place and may be established as having done so through evidence that is relatively trustworthy. Professor John Marsh in his commentary on St. John's Gospel, provides us with two very helpful English phrases as a way of making this distinction. He speaks about "what happened" and about "what was going on." In the former, "what happened," the reference is to the presumed observable occurrence, reported with greater or lesser accuracy and commending itself to us because it is in the order of factual event. In the latter, "what was going on," the reference is to what the evangelist believed God was doing in these events, the significance in some supreme sense which the evangelist found in the occurrences, whatever they were, about which he had at hand traditional material to which he could and did refer.

There are other ways in which the same distinction may be made. We might speak of "reportage," on the one hand, and of "interpretation," on the other. We might wish to say "fact" and "value"—although I am not sure that this ought to be done unless our philosophical conceptuality will allow us to do so, since all too often people use the word "value" in a rather airy fashion, as if "values" subsisted in some ethereal realm which has nothing to do with the hard factuality of experience in the world of event. The conceptuality assumed and argued for in this book will permit the use of "fact" and "value"; but it remains for us to show how and why this can be done. Certainly, in my opinion, it is dangerous to suggest by "value" some quasi-Platonic "ideal realm" when we are talking about history and Christian faith. We may find ourselves back in the fairy-tale position in respect to the supposed origins of our faith. But some distinction we must make, in some fashion or other; if we do not, we shall be mixing our speech in such a way that we may be led astray and others may be confused or uncertain about what we intend to say.

I have spoken indirectly of "scientific history." Yet one may well raise the question whether or not historical study can ever be genuinely "scientific" in the common acceptation of that adjective. Much will depend upon our definitions here, of course.

49

Obviously, historical enquiry is not like the work carried on in a physics laboratory, neither does it resemble the kind of study which is undertaken by a biologist or a zoologist. It is not similar to the work of a field scientist either, since he has before him the material with which he is concerned. In an influential series of writings Dr. Marc Bloch, a distinguished French historian, has argued that there is indeed a sense in which history may properly be styled "scientific," but he has also indicated that to speak of it in this way requires recognition of the specific and peculiar categories, methodology, evidential characteristics, etc., that are appropriate to the material with which the historian is engaged.

It is legitimate to use the word "scientific" in this entended sense, just as it may be thought legitimate to speak of theology as a "science," in the manner of Dr. Alan Richardson. Yet some of us feel more than a little hesitant here. The words "science" and "scientific" have acquired, thanks to long usage, a particular significance which derives from the so-called "natural sciences" and the related types of enquiry which may include psychology and sociology. When we strain the meaning of a word in familiar use we run the risk of suggesting that it has much the same basic point in every area where it is used. The only way in which this would be true for the word "science," some of us think, would be by taking its definition as ordered knowledge which seeks to describe certain phenomena through appropriate categories of explanation. This is not unlike the way in which *scientia* was used in an earlier day. But most people do not mean just this when they use the word today. I myself have an uncomfortable feeling that by calling theology a science and by speaking of historical enquiry as scientific one is unconsciously seeking to obtain for these disciplines the *kudos* or favorable reputation which is almost universally accorded the natural sciences and their close relations. I ask the reader to observe that I have carefully used here the adverb "unconsciously," for I am convinced that those who take a position different from the one here urged do so in all good faith and without any *arrière-pensée*. Nonetheless, I cannot help thinking that they are unwise.

Furthermore, as some recent writers have said, historical enquiry is, in certain respects, more art than science. Even in the *historie* aspect, historical enquiry requires a great deal of imaginative insight or empathy—a term that is derived, interestingly enough, from art criticism and the philosophy of aesthetics where it is used to denote that kind of sympathetic entrance into a work of art which enables the viewer to feel somehow identified with its message or its intention as the artist himself purposed it. In history, surely, the good scholar will not be content merely to list dates or names; he will try very hard to see something of what these dates and names are all about. When he is trying to reconstruct the happenings of a given period—to use our earlier examples, the Norman Conquest or the signing of the American Declaration of Independence—he will make every effort to get inside the period, to see it not as a isloated event (for no events are just that) but as a richly complex occurrence with many various contributing factors from the past that led to it, the circumstances in other places and related times, and the consequences which have followed it.

Now this point comes very close to the position which many writers on the philosophy of history today have adopted. They tell us that historical study is primarily the attempt of the scholar to identify himself with the "lived experience" about which he is to write. It is essentially the awareness, with as much sympathy as he can muster, of what it felt like to be a man living in that period. The good historian, as distinguished from the hack, will be one who will get the feel of the period in question; in a way, he will live in that period during the time he is engaged in his study. The documents which are available, the deciphering of inscriptions or their interpretation, the consideration of archaeological remains, and everything else available to him as evidence, will be preparatory to and in subordination under his main purpose, which is precisely this imaginative and sympathetic living in the period. One need not subscribe to some idealistic theory of knowledge, so far as one's epistemological presuppositions go, in order to see that such a way of working is far more likely to give one a real grasp of some event in the past, or some series of occurrences long ago or fairly recently, than "cold objectivity." In the latter case, one may have all the facts available, in the vulgar sense of dates and names, but yet fail quite completely to make the event or events a meaningful happening in the on-going course of human experience.

A number of experts would go even beyond this interpretation of history. They would agree with an old teacher of mine who years ago remarked, quite incidently, that for him "history is the story of how we got the way we are." That is, they would say that historical enquiry, at its best, is an attempt to discover the way in which the culture, society, nation, group, church (whatever it may be) to which, for one reason or another, we belong came to be the sort of thing it is. The way in which it did become is obvious enough through that which happened to it, in it, and around it, in the years before we came upon the scene. To understand something of that becoming will enable us to grasp better what this culture, society, nation, etc., really is and what is its importance for us who today share in it. Perhaps this view could be called "anamnetic," recalling that the Greek word *anamnesis* means remembrance of the past in the profound sense of knowing that past in the present. The historians who take this line claim that it illuminates their work, gives it a point and value, and opens up possibilities of relationship with present experience that do much to redeem the inevitable moments of dry-as-dust study of documents and the like. In any event, it is clear that such a view is far removed from the notion that history is identical with annal and chronicle. And the same may be said of most modern thinking on the subject.

In saying this, however, we need to avoid falling into the opposite error of minimizing the importance of what many of us were brought up on: lists of the dates of kings and battles and similar dull material. The kings and the battles have to be known, to prevent the historian from indulging in flights of fancy that are not so much imaginative as fantastic and silly. Nor can we assume that the newer ideas deliver us from dependence upon the "happenedness" of the historical; the past is the past and it is desirable, and in Christian thinking necessary, to know as much as possible about what Marsh calls "what happened" before we begin to talk freely about "what was going on." Yet having said this, some of us who suffered from the data method of teaching of history could have profited greatly from the newer approach.

Perhaps I may be personal here. As a young adolescent, I spent a good deal of time memorizing dates and names. I suppose it did not do me any harm, although it was a terrible bore and I saw no point in the exercise. "Sacred studies" consisted very largely in learning the names of the kings of Judah and Israel, and before those kings, tracing, in ways we now know to be inaccurate, the travels of the Jews on their way from Egypt to Canaan. When we came to the New Testament, I charted and then tried to commit to memory the routes taken by St. Paul on his missionary journeys, although no reason was given why I should have been obliged, along with my fellow students, to think that these journeys mattered much. I did learn a good deal about the geography of the eastern Mediterranean basin; but that is about all. But suppose that the whole business had been taught with the idea of helping the student see why, in some very important sense, St. Paul had bothered to travel at all. Suppose we had been assisted to see how the faith of the Jewish people developed, with the main stress not on dates and names but on the way in which the Jews regarded themselves as somehow chosen by God and why they did so. The splitting up of Jewry into two kingdoms could have been grasped as having antecedants in earlier experiences and consequences of a fateful sort afterward; and later events would have had their place as following upon and to a large degree conditioned by the different types of leader, the surrounding nations, the pressures upon the Jews from other peoples, etc. And when we came to the "life of Jesus," how much different would have been our appreciation of the stories we read in the gospels, if we could have been led to grasp the fact that these were told in order to bring us, like other Christians in other ages, to a deepened awareness of, faith in, and obedience to the one about whom the gospels were speaking.

To engage in such reminiscence may not serve any useful purpose, but to me at least it points out the very great value in the kinds of understanding of the historical enterprise which are now generally accepted. I do not wish to dismiss offhand what Robin Collingwood called the "scissors and paste" study of the past; already I have indicated why I think this dismissal is unfortunate and indeed impossible. But I do believe that we shall profit by bringing *historie* and *geschichte,* to recur to the distinction orginated by German historians, very close together.

How then are we to understand history and what are we to mean when we speak of it? In the light of our discussion up to this point, we can say that we need to distinguish between but never separate "what happened" and "what was going on"—or, if you prefer, "reportage" and "interpretation" or "fact" and "value." The basis for this view will be shown later in this chapter, when we come to consider how the process conceptuality helps us in our present task. For the moment I wish to urge that we need to be very clear about the difference in meaning of the two words, "distinction" and "separation." These words are frequently confused in popular speech and even in some theological discourse where one has heard quite learned scholars talk as if to be distinct from something is the same as being separated from it, which, of course, is nonsense, and which some familiarity with and use of the Chalcedonian definition of the person of Christ might have avoided.

Let us note first that in that famous definition it is said that in Jesus Christ there are two "natures," one human and the other divine. The two are united, we are told, in such a manner that they are distinct (that is, distinguishable) one from the other but they are never separated. One is always with the other, yet it is not the other. Whatever we may think of this mode of defining the Incarnation, the careful use of the terms is significant. In many areas of theological discussion, they can provide a useful guide—between divine grace and human freedom, for example, or between the Church as "the Body of Christ" and the Church as an observable sociological institution or community. Plainly this is not the place to pursue the subject in its other aspects, but the recognition of the difference between these two words can help a great deal in our seeing the relationship of *historie* and *geschichte*. For us, the point is that when we make, as we must, a distinction between history as the reporting of presumably ascertainable facts (in principle ascertainable, at least) and history as the communication of meaning or interpretation or "value," we need not, and I should urge we must not, separate the two as if they had nothing to do with each other. Nor can we really do this, however much we may try. For there are no facts that do not have some significance, however minimal this may be; while significance or value which does not rest upon some basis in factuality is in the realm of fancy. Yet we sometimes hear talk about bare facts and sometimes, although not often, about values which have no contact with the hard realities of event. There have been some who have thought that they could write an account of Jesus of Nazareth with no reference to what the gospels show as to how he was "received" and understood; and there have been some faith-judgments which have presumed that no grounding in actual life is required.

An illustration of the former error is hardly required, but the latter manifests itself in such subtle forms that one may be given. I have heard a distinguished theologian say that although there was no adequate evidence to validate the historical-biological virginal conception of Jesus and very imperfect evidence for the "empty tomb" aspect of the Resurrection, nonetheless, both the Conception and the Empty Tomb must be held as historical events for the simple reason that they fitted into, were consistent with, and had provided an enormously important setting for the doctrines of the Incarnation and the Resurrection.

For some of us, the conclusion of the matter is that any sound understanding of the meaning of history must include both elements or aspects. The mere record of the past, validated so far as may be, is of interest to some people in the same way that the lists of kings and battles are of interest. But for the Christian this can hardly be said to constitute the real historical quality of the faith to which he subscribes. On the other hand, accounts of what people have believed and valued are also interesting to some scholars and are in certain respects very important for everyone. But for the Christian, at least, these can hardly be said to constitute what he means when he speaks of his faith as historical. Both sides go together and belong together. The real meaning of history, especially as a Christian would see it, but also for others who wish to deal faithfully with the subject, must be some factual material with an interpretation or significance which is somehow communicated in the very relating of the event aspect itself. In other words, history, as we must look at it for our understanding, in fact-with-meaning.

Naturally nobody must, of necessity, think that the meaning which has been found in and drawn from the fact is the correct one; abstractly speaking, there could be a number of different meanings. What does matter is that we almost always, if not always, have to do with facts that have such a meaning attached, so to say. Yet to put it in that way is not satisfactory, since it may suggest that the meaning side is loosely or arbitrarily added to factual data which originally had no such quality. To think in that way would be a mistake. Whatever comes to us from the past, once we get beyond the mere listing of names and dates (and sometimes even when we have such listings to deal with), comes to us with some meaning. It has been remembered and handed down to others for some purpose. It has some "value," however slight that may appear to be.

Now from one point of view it might be said that such

meaning is read into what has happened. But from another, and I believe more profound, point of view, meaning is read out of what has happened. By this phrasing I am urging that nobody looks at events which have somehow been experienced by him or related to him, without some degree of evaluational activity on his part; yet this is not a purely subjective affair. Perhaps some very insignificant datum may be taken as it stands, without any sense made of it; but I am inclined to think that instances of this sort are relatively few. Certainly any happening that has been handed down for a long period, hence deemed worthy of being remembered, will have some aura of interpretation about it. As I have just said, there was a reason for its being remembered at all, however minimal may have been the significance which somebody or a community of people, may have found there—at least it had enough importance and hence enough value to be worth bothering with. Otherwise it is hard to see how it would have been written down or handed on by word of mouth or in some other way passed along to other persons, whether contemporaries or those who live long after the purported event occurred.

In the last few paragraphs, words like "significance," "interpretation," "meaning," and "value" have been used synonomously. Perhaps this was wrong, since the difference between subjective evaluation and objective significance may have been overlooked. On the other hand, a sound epistemology, in my judgment, will not be prepared to make the sharp split often proposed between the two. All evaluation is a relationship between two things: the object being discussed and the significance found in it and thus placed upon it. This may be only another way of insisting on the relation of *historie* and *geschichte,* but it has far-reaching implications. To put it in the language which seems most suitable for our purposes, all fact possesses some value. We shall need to speak of this in more detail later; here we need only remark that while perhaps sometimes people talk of value floating free in the air, with no contact with things in and of this world of occurrences, this is quite rare in serious discourse. One can assume that such speculative, theoretical, abstract talk of "value" is not common among ordinary people but is much more likely to be found among those whose philosophical interest has been of the "idealist" type. We need not deny that the tellers of fairy-tales do much the same, but then they make no pretence to be talking in other than a fanciful way. Most of us most of the time come to make valuational judgments through contemplating something which has taken place in our experience or about which we have good reason for confidence in its having happened. We find in that something a value good or bad, great or small. Otherwise we should hardly bother very much about it.

If what has been urged comes anywhere near the mark, then we can say that the historian is a scholar who is concerned with understanding the past, not only for its own sake as a series of events which once occurred, but also and more seriously for what the past has to tell about the way in which men believed, the interpretation of life which was theirs, and the values they esteemed—and also to bring out what to him seems the persisting importance, meaning, significance, or "value" of the material with which he is dealing. The fact that historians generally write essays or books in which they speak about times past is an indication that they have still another interest in pursuing their work. They wish to tell us, their readers, what in their judgment these interpreted events amounted to; they wish to tell us this because they believe that in telling it they will awaken in us a response to those interpreted events which will be of some significance today. I am not suggesting, of course, that a proper historian writes in order to "edify" or to "instruct," in the pejorative sense of those words, although it is true that some writers on historical subjects have done exactly that. But I do suggest that sometimes in spite of himself the real historian is concerned with making "fact-with-meaning" meaningful to us. That implies that he feels, although naturally not always in a highly conscious way, that the meaning which he has seen as he contemplated past events (always with some valuational quality attached to them) will have its importance and interest for others and perhaps have some kind of effect upon them.

An excellent example of what I am here urging may be found in H. A. L. Fisher's fascinatingly written and informative *History of England.* In his preface the distinguished Oxford historian explicitly disclaims any intention to teach anybody anything. Indeed he affirms that he himself can find no meaning in what he has so carefully studied and so beautifully written about the past of his own country. He thought that he was writing a book that had no interpretation and that made no attempt at evaluation. Yet those who read the book when it appeared were quick to notice that what in fact its author had done was to present the entire story of England's past as leading up to and flowering in the liberal state of which he had been so distinguished a representative and during his public career as a minister in the cabinet an ardent defender. In spite of himself, Fisher was writing history with a meaning; he was writing history in order to show what it really was about; and he was, as some critics pointed out, selective in his use of facts and ready to relate them one to another in such a fashion as would make a contribution to those who read the book. In other words, a scholar who thought of himself as dealing with bare facts was in truth dealing with facts that he believed had a significance and he could not help himself here, since after all he was a genuine historian with the sensitivity and perception proper to such a scholar. For H. A. L. Fisher, despite all his claim to "objectivity," found value in the history of England in its preparation for and ending in parliamentary democracy under a constitutional monarch. Rightly or wrongly, he saw the events of the past pointing that way; they had for him that significance; and he managed to communicate this reading of the story to a vast number of sympathetic readers.

By now it is more than plain that in my view history is best understood as a combination of what I have earlier called an "anamnetic" interest and what I have described as the attempt to put oneself back into the mind and share the experience of those who have lived in a period in the past. Coupled with this, I have insisted on the need for some factual basis, made known to us through the many types of response which are represented in written and other records. All these, as I see it, belong together, and any one of them alone will not do justice to the richness of the historian's efforts nor to the usefulness of his results. Neither will one of them alone do justice to the complexity of the historical process itself. What we can expect, then, is some grasp of events, some point found in them, some sense given them because there is already some significance attached to them; and we can hope that through identification with those facts as they come to us in this way, we shall have a deepened awareness of our own place and time and find ourselves better equipped to grasp the continuities and the novelties in the event-full life of our kind. In one way, too, history prepares us for the future. It does not give us predictions about what will happen, but it assists us to see that there are continuities as well as novelties, and in doing this, history creates both the assurance that the historical process is not a chaotic mass of meaningless detail, and the readiness to accept novelty when and as it may appear.

As to the historian himself, if he is to do the sort of job which I have argued is his distinctive vocation, he must first of all be expert in the field of so-called "scientific history," by which here I mean (disliking the phrase I have used) being competent in the study of ancient documents, inscriptions, and the other relevant material. He cannot run away from the *historie* side; rather, he must be prepared to spend years of tedious work in precisely this sort of study. At the same time, he cannot be content to leave things there. He must go on to the interpretative or *geschichte* side, first by entering into and sympathetically grasping such interpretations as his own material provides for him in the very act of giving him his information, and then by himself so deeply meditating upon what he now knows and grasps that its significance, as it comes to him, speaks personally and compellingly to his own mind and spirit. And finally, as a man who lives in his own time, he must seek to see what is the bearing of that which he has learned upon the present situation, contemporary experience, and the affairs of men. If he does not have that vision of history's value he will have failed, however acute may be his skill in the scientific side of his subject.

Let us be quite clear that it is neither necessary nor possible for the historian to be continually conscious of all that I have just been saying about his work. Much of the time he will not be conscious of it at all; he will simply get on with the job. But it will have become so much a part of him that he can proceed without needing any vivid awareness of doing exactly that. He will work in the way I have indicated because he has felt, for himself, what the past can mean even if he may not be able to articulate this in any precise fashion. His style of writing, his manner of execution, his selection of materials, and his overall perspective will show what he is doing. Therefore he need not say this, time and time again. Doing his job in this way is more important than making any claims about the historian's importance and professing some set of explicit convictions about its value. In other words, as an historian he has learned to deal with history in its most genuine sense.

It will be recalled that at several places I have urged that the conceptuality provided by process thought is of great help to us in coming to terms with history. Now it will be appropriate to spell out in some detail what was intended by those remarks. Obviously this is not the place for an extended review of the conceptuality in question. I may immodestly refer the reader to my small book *Process Thought and Christian Faith* for such a sketch; and I must mention also two other admirable and readable volumes which will give an even better survey: *The Creative Advance,* by E. H. Peters, and P. N. Hamilton's *The Living God and the Modern World.* Here we need only look at those aspects of process thought which are especially relevant to our present subject and endeavor to link them with what has been said so far in this book. Even then, our treatment must of necessity be brief and suggestive, rather than an exploration in depth.

In his Ingersoll Lecture on "Immortality," Whitehead insisted that there are what he calls "two aspects of the universe, aspects which are presupposed in every experience we enjoy." Either of these "worlds," as he styles them, would be an "abstraction" if it were "considered by itself." On the one hand there is activity where the present is created by "transforming the past and by anticipating the future." We shall say more about this point in a moment. But on the other hand, activity "loses its meaning when it is reduced to 'mere creation now' "; it requires the presence of value. "Value refers to fact [the activity of the creative process], while fact refers to value"—those are Whitehead's words. The following paragraph is a continuation of that theme:

"Value cannot be considered apart from the activity which is the primary characteristic of [what Whitehead styles] the other world. . . . Thus the world of values must be conceived as active with the adjustment of potentialities for realization. . . . Value is also relevant to the process of realization in the world of activity. . . . Every fact in the world of activity has a positive relevance to the whole range of the world of value. Evaluation refers equally to omissions and admissions. Evaluation involves a process of modification: the world of activity is modified by the world of value. . . . Thus the two sides of the universe are the world of origination [creative action] and the world of value. . . . Either world can only be explained by reference to the other world." And again, a few lines later, we read, "Origination is creation, whereby value issues into modification of creative action. Creation aims at value, whereas value is saved from the futility of abstraction by its impact upon the process of creation."

What Whitehead is here trying to indicate is that in the world as we experience it there is always a coincidence of factuality and evaluation. The evaluation is not merely man's own—he speaks amusingly about that error in another book, *Science and the*

Modern World, when he says that if such a position should be maintained, the man who had rejoiced in the beauty of nature should rather have praised himself for his fine feelings, a notion that is absurd on the face of it. The value which a fact possesses is integral to the fact, as an ingredient from the persisting realm of valuation which is God in his "primordial nature" and as a contribution to the on-going of God's working in the world as he accepts it into his "consequent nature." So when we see that some entity, occasion, or event has occurred, we are bound to say that somehow or other it has a value in the totality of the creative advance.

But if this is the case, we can at once see how the contention of the earlier part of this chapter, that fact and value belong together and that historical event is always more than bare happening but rather is happening with significance, is given some grounding in the cosmic situation as a whole. To argue for this would, of course, require going through the whole case for the process conceptuality; here we need only remark that at the very least this conceptuality does make the insistence on fact-with-value more than a mere prejudice on the part of some theologians.

Another aspect of process thought which is relevant to our subject is its approach to the problem of identity. What something is, as we may put it, can be discovered by attention to three factors which are integral to all events or occasions. We must remember here that for this kind of thinking the basic "stuff" of the cosmos is energy-events, not things or substances which may be here and not there, with a location that makes them easily definable and an essential structure that does not alter as the thing or substance is exposed to or experiences pressures from outside itself. Every energy-event is a complex organic entity in which the past which has gone to compose it is always remembered, although not necessarily (and for most levels of the cosmos below man) consciously recalled. Memory, as I mean it here, is in the deep unconscious areas quite as much as in those

63

which may happen to be conscious; it is a "visceral" matter, we might say. Included in that past which is thus remembered is the initial aim or the given possibility which the entity is to make actual and thus fulfill itself. This aim, that could well be styled the vocation of every occasion, is not added to some already existing configuration of materials, themselves previous energy-events; it is given at and with the moment when the new occasion comes into existence. Here identity is found in continuity with the aim on the basis of past events.

But it is not only the past which counts toward establishing identity. There is also a continuing relationship of each event in the world with its prior and more or less proximate environment. It influences and it is influenced by what has been going on around it; it grasps and is grasped by ("prehends" is the technical term used here) all that moves in upon it or that can be within the range of its outreach. Nothing exists in isolation from everything else; but everything exists in relationship with the rest of the cosmos at the moment. Sometimes this can be felt strongly and the experience is a very striking one; most of the time it is but dimly and vaguely felt. In this sense the whole cosmos is societal or (in Whitehead's word) "organismic." All entities belong together, for they are all participant in an interpenetrative and interrelational situation. Identity is found in continuity of such relationships.

Finally, every event is moving toward its fulfillment in a future goal. The initial aim which has been accepted by the entity is being realized, positively or negatively. If negatively, there is a deviation or distortion in the routing or direction which is taken; if positively, the right decisions are being made and the routing or direction is toward fulfillment proper to the aim which has been provided. In that fulfillment in the future, the potentialities of the occasion will be realized and the contribution which the occasion may make to the on-going creative process as a whole will have been received into the consequent nature of God. For it is God who gives the initial aim, who provides the lure that attracts the occasion to make the right decisions, and who is the final recipient of all that each occasion has achieved during the course of its routing toward its satisfaction or fulfillment. And identity is also established by the aim at that subjective goal. (The word "subjective" in this discussion does not mean a purely internal decision, attitude, or view, but the fact that the particular occasion has its own given aim which it appropriates for itself and seeks to realize.)

In this abstract discussion we may have failed to show how rich and vigorous is the identity which is established. Anyone can see this for himself. As he considers himself as John Smith, he knows that he is the focusing of an enormous series of the prior activities and evaluations which constitute his past; he knows that he is in continuing relationship with other men, with the world of nature, and with the cosmos from which he has emerged; and he knows that he has some aim toward the future, however dim this aim may seem to be at any given moment. In the felt experience of selfhood, John Smith is that past, that present, and that future, as they are convergent in the moment in which he self-consciously speaks of himself as "I." It is not as if something extra were added to make that "I"—a soul or mind or spirit that comes from outside and attaches itself to the stuff of which he is composed. On the contrary, the "I" is a way of speaking about the whole complex of past, present, and future brought to a point. Man's distinctive quality is that he is aware of this, as (so far as we know) other entities or occasions are not aware of their identity.

History, we may say, is the bringing into the open, so far as possible, of the past which has gone toward making the present focus, the event or experience as known, what it is in this moment as it moves toward the future. In doing this, the present is illuminated, while at the same time the direction of future advance may become clearer and more available because something of the general movement or routing has been grasped. I stress the word "direction" because it would be wrong to think that what has been is determinative of what will be. There is an openness toward the future, thanks to the free decisions which an occasion must make. There is the possibility of novelty through such decisions. That is, there is in the total process an element of indeterminacy in which, through choices which are made, new possibilities are made available and new ways to intentional goals may be discovered. All this is contained within a continuity in the process itself, since God both sets the limits to avert chaotic or anarchic results and constantly lures everything toward its proper fulfillment—although he does not dictate the decisions to be taken nor interfere with the freedom which belongs to the created occasion. History shows this continuity with the past and the possible projection into the future which will most adequately tend toward actualization of the present possibilities. But it also awakens us to the fact of novelty in the past, where all has not been predictable and certainly all has not been predetermined; in making us see this about the past it stimulates us to expect further novelty in the future, while it urges us to be open in the present to the opportunities that are provided for us to make sense of and find value in our contemporary existence. In this way, we are enabled to make responsible decisions now, knowing that they count both for ourselves and for others, as well as for the whole movement of creative advance and hence for God himself.

We have been speaking of high-grade organisms, namely of conscious human beings who are personalities-in-the-making. But we must not forget that such persons are societal, belonging to and participant with their fellow men. Hence their decisions are contributory not only to their own coming to be, as they work out negatively or positively the initial aim or vocation given them. These decisions also affect others in society. They may be reckless, selfish, unintelligent, in which case they may do harm; they may be generous and responsible so that they will do good. The way in which a response is made to relevant possibilities is a matter of responsibility for the conscientious man. There is always some response to the lure which is attracting the occasion toward the richest possible self-realization. But there should also be responsibility, by which I mean here the awareness of an obligation so to decide, among the relevant possibilities, that others will also benefit and be aided toward their proper self-realization. Thus a greater and more widely shared good may be achieved in the social group, a good which will contribute to a greater and more widely shared good in the creative advance as a whole and to God as the chief causative agent and the ultimate receiver of all accomplished good.

What we have said about history is applicable to the social process as focused in the community of men, in their cultures, and groups, and churches. And the contribution of history to man-in-the-making in his societal belonging (which is as much himself as his physical body) is to bring vividly before the group how it has come to be and why, the significance of decisions and commitments made in the past, the nature of its particular life or existence as a routing or direction in the advance of the creation; and by doing this to bring that past into the present so that new and responsible decisions may be made which (although often novel in their own way) will be in line with the development which has established the identity of the group for what it is. This seems to me to be a more abstract way of saying exactly what has been argued earlier about the relationship of *historie* and *geschichte,* about events in the past and their integral significance or meaning, about the amamnetic quality of historical enquiry, and about the communal nature of the Christian appeal to that which has occurred or happened—we may recall Marsh's "what has happened" and "what was going on"—as being in a genuine sense an activity of God toward his children. Further, we have spoken in such a way that it ought to be clear enough that the past is not a denial of future openness and possibility, but an invitation to adventure and risk.

The whole creative advance, including the historical and the "natural" levels, is to be understood as "historical" in the sense that there are significant happenings which alter situations and produce novelty. At the lower levels, including electrons, atoms, molecules, non-living matter, etc., this is indeed the case, although it is not a matter of observation, nor is the quality and degree of historical movement there so vividly and consciously apprehended. Yet what applies to man, as he comes to discern his own dynamics, is equally true of the world at large; otherwise we are dealing with a chaos, not a cosmos. But in man, history becomes a consciously experienced factor; one might say that the degree to which that factor is experienced and appreciated in such a conscious manner largely determines the degree to which a particular level may properly be called "human." Certainly it is the case that such an awareness is determinative of a culture or social group. As Whitehead remarked, the physicist studies low-grade organisms, while the biologist and the psychologist study organisms of a higher grade; yet in one sense they are all dealing with what goes on in ways that are analogous one with the others. Historical enquiry concerns itself with the study of such organisms, whether what we call "personal" or "social" (that is, groups), especially as they are related to the structures which give shape to the dynamics of the creative movement forward. Hence we have to do with the nation or the people of which persons are members and with culture or patterns of belief and action, as well as with appreciative and moral norms which have emerged in the course of events. Here again we find a close association between what process thinking tells us and what the more modern understanding of history has to say.

We are concerned with Christian faith and the question of history. If our line of thought has been sound, we can claim that the purpose and meaning of history, or the study of the past, is the opening up, for the community of faith, of the events which have given it its existence. Here is the bringing into the present of actions consequent upon decisions and conveyed with a value that is integral to their very factuality. They have contributed to the stance or position which the Christian Church now makes its own. This history is not merely a matter of satisfying intellectual curiosity about how the Christian faith came first to be held, through an analysis of the supposed course of events in Palestine in the first century of our era. This aspect is to be set in a wider context, although it must never be disregarded or minimized. More important than such information is the way in which the contemporary Christian community is brought to understand itself, its value being made clear as it was and where it was first known. The historical awareness provides the assurance of continuity which enables responsible decision to be taken now, with the aim of furthering the community's deepest intention and implementing and expressing the themes which the past has handed on to the present and which the present, accepting these and moving forward from them, can take into the future.

Perhaps the point of this chapter may be illuminated from a field which at first glance is very remote from our present subject. A man who undertakes a course of interviews with a depth psychologist is helped to know himself as he is today through his becoming more aware of himself as he was in earlier years. Incidents which he may have forgotten, so far as conscious memory is concerned, are brought to light, while other incidents of which he was well aware are now seen in a new light. If he can be led to accept the past for what it was, he will find it possible also to accept himself in the present and will be enabled to make decisions toward the future which will be for his more adequate, yet freely chosen, self-realization. The analogy is not to be pressed of course; like all analogies, it is but indicative and suggestive, not exhaustive or inclusive. It does show, however, something of the importance of the historical or remembered aspect of existence; and it may help us to see how the present moment is so largely dependent upon the past. Further, a consideration of the analogy may redeem the historian's work from apparent triviality, since even the least obviously significant incident in a man's past experience may be profoundly important in having been effectual, in some hidden way, in bringing him to his present situation. The same may be said with respect to the Christian community as a whole. Apparently insignificant moments, dimly recalled and imperfectly reported, may have had remarkable effects that were not grasped and appreciated at some earlier time. This is why the study of the history of the Christian Church can be an exciting and thrilling task for those who are prepared to take the trouble to engage in it.

CHAPTER 4

The Historical Nature of Christianity

We have said that Christianity is an historical religion in that it centers its faith, and worship, and life in a figure who lived at a particular time and place, a Man whose historical factuality is not in question even if the details of his actions and teachings in Palestine are not as clear and certain as we might wish. We have also said that Christianity is an historical religion in that it is a faith and life conveyed to us today through an "historically" conditioned community which we call the Church, a community which, like all other sociological groups, has its own special quality open to enquiry by scientifically minded people, but which is also in some significant fashion conscious of itself as being "the Body of Christ," whose past is ploughed into the series of events which constitute human existence in the world and is conveyed (as the Church believes) through the ages by a living memory in which the happenings from which it arose are made a living present reality.

We have also noted that when we refer to history we indicate more than the fact of past occurrences. We are speaking of the past as it is known in the present, as it shows how the given society or culture got the way it is; and we intend to assert that this appeal to history is much more than a matter of intellectual curiosity. It is a matter of life and death, for everything depends on it so far as the Christian fellowship is concerned. Yet the facts of past happenings do not come to us as bare and uninterpreted facts. We know about them because they meant something of the greatest importance to the first witnesses. But even more profoundly true, those facts, like all facts, cannot have happened without their having some value. Here the process conceptuality has assisted us by making plain that "the world of fact" and "the world of value" are never utterly separated, however distinct may be the two, one from the other. Indeed, we might even say that the distinction, in this respect, is mostly for those who wish to study the past, since in concrete reality as men encounter it, Whitehead's point is surely correct: all facts have value and all value known to us inheres in fact.

These various points are not to be regarded as a simple accumulation of statements. The truth is that the various senses of history so far mentioned belong together. And particularly for our purpose in this chapter, we need to see that because Christianity is a positive religion, it must be deeply immersed in the happenedness of the world and of the cosmic process as a whole. Thus the factual side of Christianity is placed in and finds its point through its being part of a general on-going of affairs. The world is constituted in that way and the Christian enterprise is no exception to the wider law of social process.

Sometimes it has been said that Christianity might perfectly well survive if for some reason its factual basis, in the sense of event in the past, had to be given up. During the period when the "Christ-myth theory," to which we made reference in Chapter 1, was held by a few well-known scholars, certain theologians were prepared to accept the view because they regarded it as irrelevant to what they called "the truth" of the Christian position. Naturally a good deal of reconstruction in the traditional theology might be required, since for so long Christianity has depended upon assertions made regarding a supposedly factual event. But after all, it was urged, the teaching attributed to Jesus in the gospels could still be true, even if it had not come from the lips of a real man but had been attached to a fictitious lay figure. Furthermore, it was said, a considerable amount of traditional Christian doctrinal belief could be retained, although the figure of Jesus would serve merely as an imaginatively constructed symbol of this belief. For example, Christians assert that God has "come into human life" in the person of Jesus, in a special and decisive fashion. But it might be said that God is always coming into human life in exactly the way this has been claimed of Christ. No particular instances, no special occasions, are required to make this true. The traditional conviction that in the event of Jesus Christ, God has acted redemptively for men could be generalized as a statement of God's continual redemptive activity in the world.

Now there is just enough truth in this view to make it highly dangerous. If, as we have urged, what Jesus reveals and effects as a factual event in the world's history is a disclosure of what God is always up to in the creation, it might seem of little importance whether or not the historical factuality of Jesus is stressed and it might be thought that in any event he is but the chosen instance or example of a general reality. The difficulty here is that many forget that men require specific instances, vivid occasions, and illuminating foci if they are to come to grasp truth. The point of the historicity of Jesus is that here, in that place, at that time, in that man, there is a disclosure which does not contradict but rather confirms and corrects other intimations and knowledge of God and his ways with men. Without such a focus, the quickening power of the truth there manifested would be lost. Humans are creatures of the particular, the definite, the concrete; they do not live by, nor can they give allegiance to, abstract truths and generalized propositions.

Those who took the view just criticized were often disciples of the German philosopher Hegel. They granted that the story of Jesus was a mythological account of something of enormous importance but the historicity of the event was irrelevant. The myth told the truth; that was the significant matter. Others who did not go quite so far entertained at least the possibility of this dissociation of meaning from fact; if worse came to worst, they could make do with the situation. There was a more evangelical version of this view, too. It could be said that since Jesus is represented in the gospels as teaching and exhibiting in his life the love of God, man's brotherhood, and a life with an eternal quality even if it must be lived in time, these are the essential Christian affirmations. That Jesus both asserted them and lived them out is interesting; it provided the occasion for the first glimpse of the truth; but it is not absolutely central. The "essence of Christianity" is elsewhere. Such was not the view of the great German historian and theologian, Adolf von Harnack, whose book *Das Wesen des Christentums* was translated as *What is Christianity?* Harnack was a vigorous defender of the historical factuality of Jesus and he was convinced that the gospel of Jesus required some version of a gospel about Jesus. Often he was misrepresented and some who professed to be his disciples went far beyond anything that he had wished to say when he spoke of God's fatherhood, man's brotherhood, and eternal life in the midst of time as the very heart of the Christian message.

The Christ-myth theory was preposterous and was soon shown to be so, not only by Christian scholars like Harnack himself but by semi-detached scholars like Alfred Loisy and non-Christians like F. C. Conybeare. We need not concern ourselves with it since no reputable historian holds it today. But the way in which some reacted to it is illuminating, since it shows that men of goodwill and great intelligence, like the theologians just mentioned as seeking to get on without any appeal to past event, can quite completely fail to appreciate the basic quality of the Christian enterprise. Another reaction to the theory, and indeed to all careful and scientific study of the New Testament, has been equally mistaken, however.

Those who have taken this second line have urged that since Christianity does depend on fact in the past, it also requires that we accept as they stand the gospel narratives. These are the fundamentalists and the neo-fundamentalists—the latter those who are not biblical literalists but who insist that the motifs of biblical writing and the historical factuality of all occurrences reported in the gospels (even if in some few details there are contradictions or discrepancies) must be taken by any true Christian as absolutely essential. The theologian mentioned earlier, who insisted that even if critical enquiry could not substantiate the virginal conception and empty tomb, yet the historical factuality of these two must be accepted because the Church taught them, because theology required them (in his opinion), and for the additional reason (which was not noted before) that the New Testament in his judgment asserted them, would be a case in point.

We have made it plain that some genuine factual basis is necessary if Christianity is to continue to be anything like itself as shown in the past. There is just that much truth in the remark of a wily French ecclesiastic, asked what might be done to give vitality to a French religious cult called "theophilanthropy": "You could get yourself crucified and rise the third day from the dead." The point is simple. The power of Christianity rests in its assertion that something actually did happen in the realm of human affairs which has given validity to the claims of Christian faith. Even the teaching of Jesus, unless said by somebody who had lived and had also lived out what he said, would be at best a set of moral imperatives without real grounding; while there would be the even worse possibility that it might come to be seen as only the fancy of men who were deluding themselves about how the world really goes.

What are we to say, then, about all this?

First of all, the comment made earlier about the kind of language used in Christian talk about origins in a past event is to be noted. The language is "mythological" in quality, if by this we can be understood to mean poetical, metaphorical, symbolic, rather than prosaic, literal, or exact. It is also the case that in one sense (but I think only one) the word "myth" might appropriately be used to describe what Christian have to say about this historical past. The assertion that in Jesus Christ the Son of God "was made flesh" and that this happened "for us men and for our salvation" is an assertion which tells a story, as I must phrase it, that accompanies and gives the final interpretation of another story that is strictly an account of an event in the past. My argument is that when and as we give the interpretation a Christian must give to "what happened" at a given time and place—namely in Palestine in the years approximately 7 B.C. to A.D. 27—and thus seek to proclaim "what was *really* going on" in that happening, we can do so only by using the language which belongs to drama and saga, not by using the idiom ordinarily employed for speaking of past events and their value. Here a value of a quite supreme sort has been added to the value, or type of value, which occurrences necessarily possess. Thus the introduction of God into the picture has demanded of us a heightening of the dramatic content and language.

But I hasten to add that I do not much like the admission I have been obliged to make. We must use language drawn from human experience, human contacts, and human relationships to speak of anything whatsoever. After all, men are human and they cannot speak in divine terms. No human being could conceivably say anything about God and his ways in the created order, save in language that was originally intended to speak of his own human and this-worldly experience and thought. We stretch the common significance of language; we use it to point to that which is beyond human and this-worldly experience and thought. In so doing, we hope to point to, to indicate, even to describe (humbly and hesitantly, to be sure) what God was doing in what happened. This is certainly the case; yet I still have a feeling that the word "myth," which I am allowing in this one sense, is not a fortunate one and I still prefer my suggestion in *The Word Incarnate* that "saga" is a better word.

Even in the "ages of faith," however, it was agreed that all talk about God is different in type from other discourse. Hence the univocal language which might be appropriate in much of such discourse must be replaced by the analogical language which while allowing for some overlapping levels of meaning yet seeks always to point humbly to the *altitudo*—the "beyondness" which is intended when we talk of God. There have been some who refused to talk of God at all, precisely because of the inadequacy and imperfection of our speech. I believe these have been mistaken, since their position can give rise to the idea that human reflection is unable to come to any genuine and valid apprehension of the "beyond"—this negative sort of mystical approach is to be contrasted with the Christian affirmative attitude, based as it is on the belief that God has made himself known to us, in our human terms and at our human level, in the incarnate Lord and also elsewhere. And, of course, there are those who will not speak of God because they think that in our time the word has lost its meaning altogether. These too, in my judgment, are mistaken; in their case the error has come from identifying the word itself with a certain set of stereotypes (absolute dictator, unmoved mover, eternal and absolute substance, moral dictator) which for many, if not all, of our contemporaries are rightly to be rejected.

I have no doubt that when Professor John Knox, to give one example, argues for the retention of the word "myth," he is intending to say much the same as I am saying. I believe that his discussion in his small volume, *Myth and Truth*, is invaluable and I concede the point which he has made in commenting on my own view. When we tell any story about how God and man are related we tell it in other than a literal way and yet we have references in mind to that which has actually occurred. Perhaps the way to reconcile his argument for "myth" and my dislike of it would be to speak of two stories which the Church has to tell about Jesus Christ. This would bring us close to Marsh's position, incidently: "what happened" and "what was going on." One story would be whatever we can say about the factual existence of a man who lived in Palestine two thousand years ago, what he is remembered to have said and done, what happened to him as this could, in theory at least, have been observed and set down by a reporter. The other story would tell of what God was doing there and then, as Christians have discerned this with the eyes of faith; it would be the story of the purpose and results of "the act of God," as the Bible would phrase it, which Jesus himself is taken to be. Yet the two stories would coincide in that they would both be centered in that one Man in his concrete actuality as an event in the time series in which we men have our existence.

This chapter has for its subject the historical nature of Christianity. The very title assumes that there is something which can be known by that name "Christianity." There is a continuity of the Christian "thing" throughout the years from the first to the twentieth centuries. If that be the case, then the historical nature of the Christian enterprise requires the factuality for which I have argued but which (as has been seen) I do not consider the only meaning of history. If there had been no grounding in concrete facts of human existence for what Jesus is claimed to have said; if there had been no human life about which the beliefs of Christians have been interpretations, then Christianity as a continuous and identifiable enterprise would be finished. Furthermore, even if something might possibly survive the wreckage, it would be more like a speculation, a theory, perhaps even a fairy-tale, lacking any genuine cutting edge and in no better case than the accounts of "savior-gods" in the mystery-cults of the early centuries. And if it were claimed that at least the value of the ethical teaching attributed to Jesus would be retained, the answer is that a religion would have become an ethical system. Nor would the only material we possess about Jesus, namely the New Testament (for other material is not relevant at this point), be used in a serious way. Jesus would have been at best a wiser Socrates, not the Lord and savior of men.

Christian faith is centered in and Christian life is an expression of a relationship between God and his children focused in Jesus Christ. As such a relationship, it requires an occurrence which shall have made possible just that way for God and men to come together. There must be a "given" into which others may enter. That is the genius of the Christian enterprise and St. Paul states it for us when he uses again and again the phrase "in Christ." To live in Christ, to be in Christ, to find new strength and power in

Christ, to know oneself forgiven by God in Christ—here is the heart of Christianity. Thus Christianity is neither an ethical system nor a spiritual philosophy; neither is it the quite sound belief that God and his children have a general sort of relationship one with the other. It is entrance into the God-man relationship specified in Jesus Christ, in whom what is intended to be true of all relationship between God and his children receives, through God's doing, "a local habitation and a name," and because of that, focal concretion is given coronation and fulfillment and also implementation and correction. There is something else, too. The vividness and "definition" or decisive quality of the central event has the effect of intensifying, quickening, and concentrating God's "ever present help." Through this event, something genuinely novel takes place not only in our thinking but in our human living. This is what has been intended in traditional theologies when they have spoken of "the benefits of Christ": what God has wrought in him "for us men and for our salvation."

How are we to get at and make sense of the points which have just been made? I suggest that once again the process conceptuality can come to our assistance. We have seen that talk about history is not talk about bare facts without meaning, nor bare meaning without facts. Whatever facts we know, whether of the distant or immediate past, whether in the past or in the present, we know as bearers of value. Conversely, whatever value (or meaning or significance) is known to us is known always in relationship with and communicated through something which possesses or manifests or contains this value (or meaning or significance). No ordinary person thinks that his judgments of value, his sense of meaning, or his awareness of significance are only fancies in his mind or projection of his desires and this alone. Granted that the subjective element is present. How could it be otherwise? Granted that the factual basis may seem minimal, so far as any of us is consciously aware. Nonetheless, it is there and it is more than subjective fancy. I have shown how Whitehead argued for the co-presence of fact and value, actuality and importance (or significance) as integral to every occasion or event in the world. To split the two would be to commit what elsewhere he styled "the fallacy of false disjunction," since it assumed a world of things without any human experiencing of them or alternatively a world of value (or meaning or importance) without any grounding save in a supposed subjective desire or feeling. But value or importance is always a relationship between what is seen, heard, felt, or otherwise experienced, on the one hand, and the one who thus sees, hears, feels, or otherwise experiences, on the other hand. When we say that a rainbow is beautiful we are saying that there is a relationship between certain physical events and the human apprehension of them, such that the relationship is to be characterized as an experience of beauty. This truth in the sphere of the aesthetic is a paradigm of the more general truth that fact always has value or importance and that value or importance is located in fact. Thus we return to our insistence that *historie* and *geschichte* belong together and go together; what we know in our experience is fact-with-value, not fact and value disparate and separable. They have indeed a certain distinction one from the other, but they are also inseparable one from the other.

The world we know is a world of process. It is not composed of a vast number of things that happen to be arranged in interesting or uninteresting configurations or patterns. It is composed of occurrences or energy-events, all interrelated and mutually influencing and being influenced by one another. Now I urge a further point. When some event occurs—that is, when the cosmic energies are focused or concentrated or convergent here or there—something takes place. There is novelty there; there is the appearance of what has never been exactly there before. Before that moment there has been preparation for the novelty but the novelty itself has a quality which is its own; it is no repetition of the past, even if the past is contributory to its identity. This is because the past has been brought to a point at this moment, because the various graspings (or prehensions) have here had decisions made for acceptance or rejection, and because the aim in view is here made a specific possibility in a way that has not happened before.

Not only is there novelty, however. There is an opening to the future. Each event makes a difference to the way in which things will go. The difference may be very slight indeed; but in the case of some events it may also be great. Whitehead once put this in answering a question asked him by Nels Ferré who was at that time pursuing research studies at Harvard. When Ferré asked his teacher how he would "characterize" what he styled "reality," Whitehead responded after a slight pause: "It *matters*; and it has *consequences*." The words which I have stressed make exactly the points that I have been concerned here to emphasize. "It *matters*"—that is, it is important and has value. "It has *consequences*"—that is, it makes a difference in the way things go henceforward.

Christianity in its historical concern for an actual figure who lived at a given time and place fits admirably into this scheme. Jesus lived; and Christians have found the one who lived important, possessed of value, significant. This importance, value, and significance must of course be worked out so far as their full implications are concerned. Thus Whitehead told us, in a splendid sentence, "Christ gave his life; it is for Christians to discern the doctrine." This is what has taken place. The event of Christ was received and known as having value and importance in itself as an event in the world of happenings. For those who were awakened to it, this value and importance were inescapable. Yet how could they best be expressed, in relation to God and to man? The Christian centuries have been given to finding ever deeper significance here. The event has disclosed God for what he is and does; hence in some profound way the event has its divine side. On the other hand, it has disclosed man for what he may become; hence it has its human side. The two, divine and human, are knit together in a seamless robe; hence there is a unity of God and man in the event. Then it is necessary to seek to work out how such a unity may be understood—and we have the story of the christological councils and later theological interest in what came to be called the mode of the Incarnation. But basic to the development is the initial intuition which found that in Jesus and all he was, said, did, accomplished, there was what Whitehead called "the disclosure of the divine nature and agency in the world," given in human terms so that men can be grasped by it and respond to it.

Thus the historical appeal of Christianity, in this sense of the word history, is to a figure who is taken to be among all other events the important one, with a value that is inexhaustible. This is the supreme indicative moment, for Christian faith, precisely because Jesus is not separated from his human brethren but in their concrete human situation is the classical instance of what God is doing to lure the children of men to himself, to awaken human responsivity, and to bring his love more effectively into operation in human affairs. One further comment and we must turn to the second of the primary senses in which Christianity is an historical religion—that is, its being a faith, worship, and life conveyed in a community immersed in the on-going processive movement of the human race.

The comment has to do with the risk that is involved in Christianity's basing so much upon an event in the past. There is no reason to doubt the witness of competent scholars and other experts in ancient history who assure us that the factuality of Jesus is not in question. On the other hand, there can also be no doubt that to ground the whole enterprise on such a factual event, however valuable and true may be the considerations which lead us to do so, is to take a risk. Some would like to have no such risk. These either settle for some purely mythical interpretation (in the pejorative meaning of "myth") or fall into a fundamentalism which claims that everything is quite clear and certain, questions and doubts being works of the devil. But surely there is a certain contingency about the Christian position if it is so related to past event, no matter how strong is the evidence for that event. For about no event of this kind can we claim the absolute certainty appropriate in scientific or mathematical discourse. We are dealing here with vital matters that resemble the trust of a man in his wife, the confidence of friend in friend. In such areas of human experience there is always an element of risk. Faith in God's action in Christ, because it is faith, is of the same order.

But then why should any Christian wish to deny this element of risk? Life itself always has a risky quality; we must venture beyond what we can prove and allow for contingency even when we have moral certitude. Human experience is that way and there is no reason to assume that Christian belief in the importance of Jesus Christ as the Christian community knows him is in a completely different category. There is always "the leap of faith," in Kierkegaard's words. What I have been urging is that in a sense this is a "calculated risk"; it is not a leap in the dark. There is enough evidence to make it a rational act. But if there were no such evidence, Christianity as it has been known and accepted through the centuries would no longer be a viable possibility. Something else might appear which included some of the elements of Christianity, but it would be a substitute article. It would not be Christianity as an identifiable series of occasions through which a community knows itself as a social process of a specific sort—namely, the historical Christian Church.

This brings us to the other primary sense of Christianity as historical. Not only does it have to do with an actual figure who lived at a particular time and place and about whom something is known to us, sufficient to justify the high place given to the figure in Christian faith. It is also a faith appertaining to a community ploughed into and part of the on-going processive movement of events in the world. This is the aspect of Christianity's historicity which has often been neglected by those who rightly stress the former aspect.

We may make the point by saying that there is no such thing as Christianity apart from the community or fellowship or group known to us as the Christian Church. That is to put it very bluntly. When phrased in this brief and unequivocal way the point can be difficult to understand and much more difficult to accept. For this reason the rest of the present chapter will be devoted to a development of that too simple and straightforward statement. Precisely because it can be affirmed in such a simple and apparently naive manner, it can appear ridiculous, while it also seems to overlook the patent fact that a great many people who call themselves Christians are very doubtful about the importance of any of the organized groups that constitute the institutional Church and do not make much, if anything, of their being part of the community which we designate when we use this traditional word.

The founded and positive nature of Christianity means, as we have said, the fact that the faith which Christians hold is communicated through the years by a social organism whose existence is profoundly sunk in the on-going process of events which may be called historical development. Those who think that they can be Christian entirely apart from that community are very much mistaken. It may very well be true that such persons have no formal connection with any religious group. They do not attend the worship of the Church. In externals they appear to be entirely unattached. Yet they should not decieve themselves. For they learned whatever they know about Jesus because the Christian community remembered him and has produced books (gospels, etc.) which tell about that remembrance. They practice what they would call the Christian ethic because that ethic is a formulation of the principles which the community worked out on the basis of what it knew of the teaching of Jesus in the context of other moral ideas in the Greco-Roman world. Very often their belief in God, however they may conceive of him, is a relic or vestigium of convictions held by the Christian Church. In all these senses they are much more dependent on the Christian community through the ages than they may have recognized to be the case.

Can this supposedly detached Christianity continue long unless there is a community to support it? This is a very important question in our own day. Certainly great generosity and goodness, the participation in the struggle for social, economic, political, and racial justice, and the concern for truth are found among many who do not think they require the community. In this way such persons put "church-people" to shame. Their very revolt against aspects of traditional Christian theology and apparent moral negativism is impressive—much more so than the bovine acquiescence of numbers of active (or "passive"!) churchmen in what they have been taught and about which they may show no critical concern. But all these things may very well be a reflection or, sometimes a negative reaction to, what the community has seemed to say. A negative reaction is, in itself, an indication of some sort of dependence upon that which is critized. Furthermore, much of professedly humanist or secularist thinking and action is a protest, not against an authentic Christian position but against perversions and distortions of that position which, from time to time, have become dominant in some sections of the community.

The fact of Christianity's communal nature is plain enough, one must think. For it is unquestioned that the faith in Christ has come down to us today through an historical community. Whether we are prepared to accept it or reject it, whether we dislike it or approve of it; whether we wish changes were made in its mode of statement and its implementation in concrete actions or feel satisfied with things as they are—we cannot avoid reckoning with its existence as a given fact in the realm of human affairs and as part of the on-going process of creation. Even the most radical critics are still affected in some way by that social process within the greater historical process. The Church is there, for good or ill.

The social process within the greater historical process is a way of looking at this particular aspect of Christianity's historical nature. We have said again and again that in the world which we know everything is in movement, including the natural order as well as the events in human existence. In a world like that, with the dynamics that characterize all occasions, the Christian community has its place. In that wider process the Church exists and lives; apart from it, the community would be an ideal "dream city," not unlike Plato's idealized Republic which is laid up in heaven but not effectively present on earth.

To speak in this way helps us to see that the historical nature of the Church is a living process. The community is dynamic, a stream of life, a continuity given identity by its remembrance of its past, its relationships in the present, and its future aim, like all other identifiable occasions. Thus we are delivered from the notion, so long held and taught, that to speak of Christianity as historical required us also to believe that there were specific established ("divinely instituted") forms which in their precise was constituted the apostolicity of the Church. For those who were brought up in other Christian groups it was very likely different, but for us who were trained in more traditional churches, the forms were rigidly and almost mechanically understood. Once again to be personal, I was brought up to believe that the only ministry which could claim to celebrate valid sacraments and exercise functions of a priestly sort was one which had come down by tactual succession through the laying-on of hands by bishops who themselves had been consecrated in a proper succession. Furthermore, the creeds, Apostles' and Nicene in particular, were required for the statement of Christian belief. Some degree of freedom in the study of their phrases was allowed, of course, but they were to be taken as all "of a piece." Indeed the right mode of interpretation was described, in a statement issued by bishops in the United States, in respect to such a possibility of study, in these words: "Fixity of interpretation is of essence of the creeds." This presumably meant that while one could interpret in the sense of rephrasing words and ideas, any deviation from the accepted theological meaning as given in the classical theologies of Catholic Christendom was absolutely mistaken and bordered on blasphemy. I was also taught that there were seven sacraments which had been instituted by Christ, either directly and specifically (Baptism and the Eucharist) or indirectly by inspiration of the Church on the basis of some act performed by Christ during his days on earth—Confirmation, Penance or sacramental confession of sins with absolution pronounced by a priest, Anointing of the sick or dying, Marriage for those called to that estate of life, and Holy Orders for those called to serve in the ministry. The ministry, creeds, and sacraments were of the very essence of the historical community; and the Bible, which was the fourth of the great forms, was regarded as proving or demonstrating what the Church taught to be the truth, without which there was no assurance of eternal salvation.

I do not wish to seem to parody the Anglo-Catholicism of my youth, for I still value highly much that I learned from it and I still believe that the Catholic way of being a Christian is closer to the social process view I am defending in this book than the idea which was at that time taught in so many Reformed churches, that Christianity is "the Bible and the Bible only." I think that in those Reformed churches there was also something resembling the static and rigid view in which I was brought up. The fashion in which this was stated and the mode of its manifestation would have been different, of course, but the ways in which justification was taught, men were held responsible for obeying the Ten Commandments, the authority of Scripture, etc., were understood, would not have been too dissimilar. Despite the freedom which the Reformation experience ought to have made possible, and in its own time did do so in reaction from the formalism of the medieval and post-medieval Catholic Church, a static conception was very generally accepted.

Now in a way we can see how this view of Christianity's historical nature as a community could have come to be accepted. For centuries, the world was regarded as a static order, in which things were here and not there; where one could speak meaningfully of definite position and status; where even God was thought to be unchanging and aseity (or self-containedness and self-sufficiency) was his "root attribute," while his love was an adjectival qualification of his absolute power. In a world like that, it was possible to think of the Christian Church in terms equally static. To speak of historical continuity must then mean, in this context, to point to definite and definable beliefs, practices, rituals, and views. If these were Catholic there would be one set; if these were Protestant, another. But the paradigm throughout was of an established and formalized ordering. Of this the ministry was an excellent illustration. The ordained man had a specific, clearly defined status in the historical structure of Christianity and he could count on this and be respected for it. And this attitude to ministry was as much found in many Reformed churches as in the Catholic churches.

We live now in a world where such fixity is taken to be nonexistent. There are identifiable structures, to be sure, but these are not the rigid and unyielding ones of an earlier time. They permit of modification and accommodation according to new circumstances, within an overarching continuity. There is novelty and there is also a continuation in process so that similarities may be noted even when we also observe differences. Cardinal Newman's famous words apply to the situation: "In another world it may be otherwise, but in this world to live is to change and to be perfect is to have changed often." Change is part of the story; yet the change is not productive of anarchy or chaos, for there are the persisting identities which enable us to say that this or that is or is not in line with the broader movement of advance from the past about which we have learned through sympathetic identification with what went on in an earlier time. Continuities are to be seen in a living social process, in which (as I have continually argued) real identity is constituted through the focusing of the past, the present, and the future aim at a given moment. Continuity is not found in a once-for-all collection of beliefs, practices, and ministry.

Another way of saying this is to note that in the world which we know function is more important than supposed location, since it is a world where activity is everywhere present and where value attaches to the events which occur. Decision is necessary in the present; but the decision is in the light of the past and it aims toward future fulfillment. So, to be aware of the historical nature of the Christian community is to be grasped by a living movement and not imprisoned in a tight box of belief and form. Within Christian circles this has meant that words and phrases which once seemed conventional are filled with new vitality. "Life in Christ," "the primacy of love," "doing the truth," etc., serve as examples here. In all these ways we are forced into what for many is quite new and sometimes distressing and disturbing.

We are also being led to grasp the fact that the neat lines of boundary which were drawn around the Christian Church can no longer be maintained. I have said that one cannot be a Christian without some dependence upon the community. But I have not said that those who are not actually affiliated with a specific Christian group are unable to be Christian in any sense. Who is a Christian? In my youth, a Christian was one who had been baptized by water (and "the Spirit"), and hence brought into the organized Church. If he was to be a fully mature Christian he was supposed to be confirmed, a practicing communicant, one who followed the disciplinary rules of fasting and abstinence and observed the "days of obligation" which were set forth by the organization. In other Christian denominations there were different requirements; but in some such way it was easy enough to say who was and who was not a Christian.

But our world is in process and the Christian community is also a social process. It is impossible to locate anything precisely here, not there, since the ramifications and affects are so wide and so vast. Many are affected who do not "belong." The structures of identity, about which we have already spoken and with which our next chapter will be largely concerned, are there since Christianity is an identifiable social process. Faith remains commitment to God's activity in the event of Jesus Christ;

worship continues to be the entrance into life in Christ through sacramental and other means; ministry goes on as representative and functional for the community in doing its work in the world; the Bible makes the formative events a present reality and enables us to test identity by appeal to the originative spirit of the community; the quality of life which manifests God's love in Christ is a constant. But all these structures may be most variously understood and interpreted, modified where necessary so far as details and form are concerned, and manifested in different ways in particular periods of man's historical existence. And some men hold the faith or live the Christian life quite "outside" observable bounds. Hence there is a freedom, a vitality, an openness, which were lacking in older Christian views.

To conclude, we repeat that the Christian Church is an historical community, embedded in a processive world. It is constantly in touch with the events which brought it into existence, for it has to do with what are accepted as facts with meaning or value. Thus the two primary senses of Christianity's historicity are brought together. We must consider how an historical event comes alive in a vital faith. This will require an examination of what seem to me the three chief activities of the community as it actually functions in the world: (1) the proclamation of Jesus Christ as "the disclosure in act," for man's wholeness or salvation, of what God is and what God does; (2) the celebration of this event of Christ through eucharistic participation in order that what is proclaimed in the Word is received in the sacrament—to put it in Luther's language; and (3) the "life in grace" which is both fellowship with God in Jesus and also external action in the world in the Spirit of Christ.

CHAPTER 5

History and the Living Faith of the Church

The Christian appeal to event in the past and the historically grounded character of the Christian community together establishs the specific and concrete identity of the social process which is known as the Christian Church. The establishment of this identity through the historical appeal and embodiment of the Christian faith is not to be separated from the achievement, in every succeeding age, of that same identity through relationships with the world of the time; nor can it be separated from the projective aim or purpose which is in view in the future—the giving by God of his kingdom for whose coming the community exerts itself in preparing and making ready the way. We have made clear the three-fold nature of identity, with its focusing of past, present, and future; this, which is true of every significant occasion is in a distinctive way true of the Christian Church. At the same time, however, the function played by the historical appeal is of quite particular importance, since for there to be a continuity which will be recognizable as such it is necessary to look to the event in the past, with its importance and value. That event, which brought into existence the community of faith, is continually remembered in the Church, not as a happening in the past now over and done with but as a happening which is conveyed to and appropriated in every present moment of the Church's on-going existence. This is what makes it possible to speak of continuity of development, characterized by certain definite factors which persist through the ages although they are differently expressed in different periods.

It is one thing to say this. Members of the Church could talk themselves blue in the face about how this identity is known and how this continuity is necessary. But words alone do not count for much in a world where "actions always speak louder than words." If that old saying has always been true, it is more obviously true for us today when we have been brought to recognize and accept what I have styled the processive nature of the world order in which activity, things that happen, events or occasions, are the very stuff of reality. In such a world "doing the truth," in the phrase from St. John's Gospel, is the way in which we can best speak the truth. What then does the Christian Church do in manifesting in action its historical identity and continuity? This chapter is intended to supply suggestions as to the way in which that question should be answered.

Put very succinctly, the Christian community manifests its identity and realizes its continuity by three activities: (1) the proclamation of the Word; (2) the celebration of the sacrament of the Eucharist, and (3) the inward and outward behavior that makes visible and available in the world the life of him whom in Word it proclaims and in sacrament celebrates. Of course these three activities do not take place in some sphere which is peculiarly "religious." They take place in the concrete world of ordinary human experience. Nothing is so likely to damage the integrity of Christianity as the notion that it must confine itself to what sometimes has been styled "the world of religion." There is no such world, as a matter of fact. The only world there is is the world of ordinary daily life; religious activities are part of that world or they are irrelevant and insignificant. So the Church proclaims the Word in the world of human affairs; it celebrates the sacrament, or should do so, not in some retreat from everyday life but in the places where the celebration can be witnessed and found meaningful; and it concerns itself with the personal relationship of men with God in Christ and the outward action which will manifest that relationship, not in an esoteric fashion appropriate to some "secret society" but in the workaday world where people actually live, do their jobs, experience joy and anguish, and know themselves to be responsible, yet finite creatures.

Furthermore, while it is the Church which engages in these activities, the agency through which it does them is the human agency of men or women who are the visible instruments for the actions. The Church is not some utterly suprapersonal society which has its ways of acting in separation from those who are its members. Such a quasi-Hegelian notion has nothing to do with the concrete existence of Christ's Body in the world. Thus when we say that the Christian community proclaims the Word, celebrates the sacrament, and lives the life in grace, we are by that very phrasing saying that its doing is through human persons. And human persons are themselves on the way to becoming men—indeed becoming persons, for they are "in the making," not finished articles. Each man, like everything else, has his processive quality, his focusing of past and present and future, and hence his mode of establishing his identity. What is more, the Word proclaimed, the sacrament celebrated, and the life lived are part of a movement toward the fullest enrichment and growth of man as he is intended to be, as well as of the society of men as that society is intended to be. The Church is like every other historical community in that it is made up of people, addresses itself in its actions to people, and performs those actions by people. Anything else we may wish to say about the Church's nature must be given concrete grounding in this obvious fact.

Thus when we speak of the Church as the Body of Christ, as I have just done, we are not suggesting some "body" floating in thin air. It is Christ's Body, to be sure; but it is that because in the concrete actuality of historical events it serves him by making his reality vivid and available. Similarly, it is true that the actions of the Church are also of God and in sacrament and prayer and worship to God. But we must reject the idea that we can have to do with God in separation from the world in which he is at work, above all in separation from the human lives in which he is at work in a distinctive fashion. Personal communion with God in Christ is a reality, to be sure, and its cultivation is a normal and proper element in the Christian enterprise. Yet for a Christian, and indeed for anyone, such a communion with the God whom we worship is no "flight of the alone to the Alone," in which God and a man may have a private tête-à-tête without any others present to interfere. If the Christian message is true, we love God in and through loving our neighbor, for it is in and through our relationship with the neighbor that God discloses himself to us—signally in *the* "neighbor," the man Jesus. We love God in and through his world, too, despite some who would refuse to accept the world as hallowed by God and intimately tied up with his movement in creation. It is through our existence in that world, not in some escape from the world, that we know whatever we do know about God.

The ancient Latin collect for the Sixth Sunday after Trinity in the Anglican Prayer book is mistranslated. The original Latin ran *amantes te in omnibus et supra omnia,* "loving thee in all things and above all the things in which we love thee." It is too bad that Cranmer in making the translation into English omitted that phrase *amantes te in omnibus* ("loving thee in all things") and hence gave the impression that it is our Christian duty to love God "above all things" without concerning ourselves with the "things," the world of creation, through which we are brought to love him. The entire Christian incarnation-sacrament outlook is a flat contradiction of any such escapist or extricationist religiosity and it is firmly grounded in the total biblical witness which finds God disclosed to men through the world in which he has been pleased to work. I say this knowing that many who are taken to be highly spiritual and peculiarly Christian have succumbed to an utterly un-Christian fallacy—usually because of bad teaching which they have received from those who ought to know better.

We now turn to the three activities of the Christian community about which we have spoken. We shall examine the significance of each of them in the light of our earlier study of the meaning of history, the Christian community's concern for the historical, and the sense in which all men are immersed in the realm of events. If our argument has been valid, a consideration of these distinctive characteristic actions should provide confirmation of what has been said; while conversely, what has been said should illuminate the activities and give them added meaning for the Christian disciple. Further, such a discussion may help to clarify the "performance" of the actions themselves, for all too often their point has been made rather incidental to the whole enterprise of Christian faith. If I am right in my thinking, the man who would be a Christian in the fullest sense of the word must somehow have his part in all three, although naturally there will be varying ways in which he plays that part.

We come first, then, to the proclamation of the Word. By this I mean primarily, in the present context, the preaching of the gospel of Jesus Christ, although the proclamation is by no means confined to sermons or other exercises of the kind. It has to do with all those activities by which members of the Christian community and those who are outside its visible boundary are confronted by the disclosure of God in Jesus Christ and thereby called upon to make or to renew their response to that disclosure. It is a call for decision, as used to be said in evangelical circles. This proclamation is an announcement of that which in Christ God "determined, dared, and did," to adapt slightly some words of Christopher Smart from *Song of David.*

Thus when any sharer in the community's life brings to bear upon others, in whatever manner he may do this, his witness to the significance of the event of Christ as God's activity for man's wholeness, making this witness in the presence of fellow Christians or of non-Christians, not to speak of the vaguely Christian people so often found in contemporary society, he is engaged in carrying on this work of proclamation. But since the most familiar way in which the proclamation is made is in the preaching of the

Church, normally undertaken by one who has been ordained for this among other functions we must speak specifically of this act.

It is unfortunate that in common usage any address given in the course of a Christian service of worship has come to be known as a sermon. We should have some way of distinguishing between the proclamation of the Word (which in my judgment a sermon properly speaking must be) and edifying discourses on moral issues, discussions of theological topics, devotional or meditational instruction, let alone that odd invention of the contemporary pulpit known as "the inspirational address." In a book published a decade ago (*Proclaiming Christ Today*), I sought to make this distinction clear. I pointed out that from the earliest days the proclamation of the gospel or Word was the reason for the pulpit and that other types of discourse, however useful or important in their place, ought not to be substituted for that preaching. I even ventured to suggest that it might be better if such discourses were delivered in some other meeting place than the actual scene of the Church's regular worship, where this was possible, so that their difference from the authentic sermon might be obvious to those who listened. If they must be given in that place of worship, I urged, it should be made plain that they were not intended to be substitutes for the regular proclamation of the Word, especially during the celebration of the Eucharist where normally and rightly the sermon belongs. More will be said about this in a moment.

What then is to be the content of the sermon, properly understood? In that same book I answered this question by saying: "The activity of God in Christ for the wholeness of man." I still believe this to be an accurate, if not entirely adequate, definition of what the regular proclamation of the Word by the Church ought to be. Its very brevity, of course, lays the definition open to misunderstanding; hence some expansion of the answer is required.

I am not urging the preaching of theology. Indeed this is

farthest from my mind. Theology is of great importance, to be sure, since a faith which has no theological articulation is likely to be without much intellectual content and thus unable to help men worship God with their minds as well as with their hearts and wills. Also I should wish to insist that any right proclamation of the Word will have about it a theological quality, by which I mean that it must be so structured, coherent, and organically related with the total import of the Christian enterprise that it is always heard in context. But to say this is not to say that theology is to be preached. On the contrary, the witness of the centuries shows us that theology is to be discussed, which is quite a different matter. In that sense, theology is in much the same position as moral discussion, devotional instruction, and the like, all of which have their proper place within the wider teaching ministry of the Church, but none of which can be identified with the gospel itself. It is very easy for a clergyman to assume that when from the pulpit of his church he has given a lecture on some aspect of Christian theology he has preached the gospel. The probability is that he has done nothing of the kind; he has been expounding the views of great theologians, perhaps his own views, about the theological interpretation of ancient credal formulae or of systematic doctrine, or at the best his views as to what the gospel suggests in terms of coherent rational ordering of ideas. But none of these is the gospel.

The "Word," as we are using it in this chapter, is that gospel, the good news of God's revealing and saving activity in Jesus Christ. Because it is this, it is also the declaration that God is as the event of Christ has disclosed him. The divine nature and agency is exactly of this quality. The preaching or *kerygma,* to use the now familiar New Testament term, is not argument about the existence of God as against atheism or unbelief. Such would be appropriate enough elsewhere and in another context. But in the worship of the Christian community the gospel is to be announced in as compelling and vivid a manner as possible, precisely because the gospel affirms that in the vivid and compelling life of a man, God as love-in-act decisively and in singular clarity declared himself. In addition, and as a natural consequence, the gospel is the assertion that when and as men respond in commitment to that event proclaimed in the preaching, they are opened to the possibility of newness of life, "wholeness," and authenticity, with the assurance of divine acceptance, forgiveness, and grace.

In language now familiar from earlier chapters, this means that the proclamation of the Word is a way in which the past event of Christ is made a living present encounter with him. It is Christ himself who speaks in the preaching; the ordained minister, or anybody else whose voice is heard, is the instrument through which that speaking of Christ is carried on. Here the Christian community renews its faith and loyalty; here it remembers, in the deepest sense, its originating source in history; here it reestablishes its identity. Of course the proclamation may be approached from many angles and may be illuminated by much material drawn from the common experiences of men. It need not be the repetition of some hallowed words in which it has hitherto been made. It need not even be by the use of the idiom natural to those who first proclaimed the gospel in the days of which the New Testament gives us the record. Precisely because the gospel is about God and God's activity in the world, it is always fresh and new; and precisely because it has reference to men and women in the contemporary world, to whom it is spoken, it must take account of their very modern questions, problems, needs, desires, and interests. What is demanded of the preacher of the gospel, if he is to perform rightly this identifying function of the Church, is careful preparation, deep commitment to the gospel itself, knowledge of the people to whom he is proclaiming it, and the ability to say simply and directly what is the point of the activity. Above all, surely, the deepest need is the conviction that God has indeed manifested himself to men in Christ.

In the Church's early days and for a long time thereafter, preaching or proclamation was part of the normal worship of the

Christian fellowship when it gathered together on the Lord's Day. There were other occasions, of course; so there will be today. There are evangelistic meetings, missions, and the like. There is also the less obvious type of proclamation which comes from a life that witnesses to the gospel although little may be said vocally about the matter. But normally the proclamation is integral to the week-by-week worship of the Church. And that tells us that the proclamation is to be embedded at the heart of the Church's celebration of the Eucharist. About that sacrament we shall speak shortly. Here it is worth our recalling that the Reformers of the sixteenth century had as their ideal for Christian worship the sacrament celebrated and the gospel proclaimed in the course of a single action. An interesting illustration of this intention is to be found in the rubric in the Book of Common Prayer where it is directed that a sermon shall be preached in the course of the Holy Communion, at an appointed place; nowhere else in the Prayer Book is such an order given. That rubric is typical of the wish of the Reformers; it has been a tragedy that for various reasons, some of them sociological, this wish has not consistently been fulfilled. It is also interesting that since Vatican II, the Roman Catholic Church directs that a sermon be preached at the chief Mass on Sundays. As the Reformed churches recover their awareness of the centrality of the sacrament, the Catholic communion is rediscovering the importance of the proclamation of the Word.

Normal Christian worship, we may say, should be eucharistic, in both meanings of that word: expressed by the celebration of the sacrament and marked by the note of thanksgiving for what God has done in Jesus Christ for men's wholeness. If this is true, then the gospel's proclamation is the occasion for celebration and thanksgiving. In some words of Martin Luther's, which we have paraphrased earlier in this book, the Word which is proclaimed in the preaching is the Word that is to be received in the sacrament. It is for Christians to appreciate their privilege and to participate in the double action every Sunday.

This leads directly to a discussion of the second of the ways in which the historical reality of Christianity as social process is made a present reality—the second of the distinctive activities by which the Christian Church manifests its identity and continuity.

Why is the Eucharist thus central? The obvious reason, to begin with, is that primitive Christians believed, and in the gospels reported, that Christ himself had commanded and taught that by this action he was to be "remembered." In itself that would be sufficient; but there is something else. The Lord's Supper is given its special place because during the history of the Christian Church as it has ploughed itself into the on-going experience of men, this action has been experienced as providing exactly what Jesus is said to have intended: a making real in the present of the living presence and the concrete achievement of Christ himself. As we have noted again and again, "remembering" here does not mean simply a reverie about events which remain as such in the past. "Remembrance" and "memory" signify the making present in contemporary experience of that which has occurred in the past—and in this instance that which has occurred to inaugurate the Christian social process which we call the Church, with its own specific identity. This is genuinely *anamnesis,* the vital reliving of the past in the immediacy of the present for those who are caught up in the action. This is what the Eucharist is all about; this is why it is one of the three essential modes of establishing Christian identity and continuity.

The word "action" has just been used about Holy Communion; and this word is important for our purposes. The narratives which tell us about the Last Supper in the Upper Room, "on the night before he was betrayed," portray Jesus as directing that something be done "in remembrance" of him. They do not tell us that he said that his disciples were to think this or that or talk about this or that. Since they were commanded to do something, the Lord's Supper is inevitably to be seen as primarily an action performed by his followers in the community of faith.

The action in the Eucharist is four-fold, as Dom Gregory Dix has pointed out in his striking book, *The Shape of the Liturgy*. There is a taking and using of bread and wine; there is a thanksgiving said over these two "elements" or natural things; there is a breaking of the bread; and there is a giving or sharing of bread and wine with those who are present. The bread and wine which are thus taken, thanked over or blessed, in the case of the bread broken, and given or shared are for the Christians who participate in this action a means by which they "receive in their hearts," as the formula puts it, the life of Christ. There have been many theories about how this is possible and the mode of the presence of Christ in the action of the Eucharist. So too there have been many theories about what the sacrament may be understood to be, in terms of the other aspect stressed in traditional formularies: "the continual remembrance of the sacrifice of the death of Christ." How can this action relate to the dying of Christ on Calvary two thousand years ago? Whatever may be the theories, the fact remains a constant in the on-going experience of Christian people. Here Christ is "remembered"—not in his dying alone, but in the totality of his life in the world, since (as St. Bernard said) "the whole life of Christ is the mystery of the Cross" or of Christ's self-giving—and here he is known as present with his people.

It is often forgotten that the symbolism of the Lord's Supper derives from a Jewish background of worship and of sacred meals. Doubtless much has also been contributed from Greco-Roman or Hellenistic religious beliefs, but it is increasingly recognized by scholars that the Jewish element is decisive. For a Jew, any strictly literal sense in which "bread and wine" become "body and blood" would have been utterly abhorrent and, indeed, incredible. But to share in the bread of the common meal and to drink together the wine which was poured for them would have meant a genuine incorporation into the life of the Lord and a way in which the true significance of his acts could be apprehended—not in the mind alone, but with the whole personality. Symbols in this sense are not only external signs which point to some reality that they have been taken to indicate, usually for reasons of conventional convenience. Rather, symbols are instrumental in effecting participation in that which is being symbolized; in a way, they are the very thing itself, although not in any literal and matter-of-fact fashion. Thus the bread and wine, set apart to be symbols of Christ's "body and blood" would stand for and would convey the whole event of Christ as historically lived out, and with that event the activity of God that was the truest depth in what was going on there. In this way, through the action of the Lord's Supper, the Christian Church is enabled (by the Spirit working through it, a theologian would wish to add, since this is no merely human action) to unite the living Lord and his people. The identity of the Christian reality of life in Christ is established afresh when the Eucharist is celebrated and the "process of Christ," in William Law's telling phrase, is known for what it is, as the disciple enters into that process and is the recipient of the "spiritual food of the body and blood of Christ."

In the action of the Eucharist, there are two directions. The Lord's Supper has a reference from God to men and a reference from men to God. Both of them are of equal importance, although the former is the precondition of the latter. So it must always be in biblically oriented religious faith: God comes first and awakens the response which is made to him. In the theologian's word, he is "prevenient," or comes before, the faith which commits itself to him. The double direction of the sacrament is typical of every aspect of the Christian enterprise. We have God's self-disclosure and man's awakening to its significance; divine grace and human freedom of response; God's forgiveness and human acceptance of forgiveness—these will serve as other examples of a paradigm given in the Eucharist and in the event of Christ which the Eucharist makes present. For the event of Christ is first God's action toward man and then man's saying the "Amen" to that action; for Christian faith the Lord himself is act of God and responding act of human life in the rich intimacy of a personal communion.

God to man: This statement, as we have just noted, is generally true in respect to the whole course of the creative process. Hence, God to man is a special case of the wider, God to the world. It is God who supplies what in process thought is known as the initial aim for each entity; it is God who lures and attracts each occasion and society to its actualization as it makes its decisions for acceptance or rejection of relevant possibilities presented to it; and it is God who is the ultimate recipient of all that is achieved by each occasion and event for the implementation of good, both for itself and for all else in the creative advance of the world. Man to God: Here once again we have a special case of a wider reality in the process of the world. Each occasion must make its own decisions, within the freedom which it possesses, so that in its response to the initial aim, the lure, and the future goal it is responsible and accountable. Further, the proper response through such decision is the one which is in the direction of the fullest possible actualization of potentiality under the given circumstances. And because each occasion is a focusing of the social or organic cosmos at that particular moment, everything in the process up to that moment, and all the environing activities which are grasped through their impinging on and influencing the choices which may be made, are involved in the decisions that are taken. The response to the invitation or solicitation of the good, whether positive or negative, is always personal at the human level but it is never narrowly individualistic.

The Eucharist is entirely in line with this more generalized truth about the way the creation goes. Here the God-to-man movement is in the recalling into the present from the past of the classical instance of God's prior activity vis-à-vis the human situation. It is a making alive now of God's intensive or concentrated action then. But in being this, it is a summation of all God-to-man movement, in the more remote past and at every point in the process and now in the immediacy of the Eucharist itself. The man-to-God movement in similar fashion is a concentration or intensification of the wider response make through decision throughout the created order, including all that has gone into the decision and its implementation in human action. What is especially significant about the Lord's Supper, however, is that the response is made, in the first instance, in the here-and-now of the contemporary worshipper's receiving. This is the faith by which, as the Anglican Article of Religion tells us, "we receive the sacrament." The faith is a response to the God-to-man movement; but without it, the sacrament would not effect the relationship between the risen Lord who is remembered and the believer who has his existence in the contemporary world. There is thus a double *anamnesis* in the Eucharist, first the bringing of the originative event into the present moment and second the remembering in faith by the believer of that which Christ has done and still is doing.

The action of the Lord's Supper is the distinctive mode of Christian worship. Obviously there are other types of worship; certainly there is the personal prayer of the faithful as they seek to align their desires with the divine desire for good and their wills with the divine purpose. Yet the Eucharist "comprehends the whole mystery of our redemption," as Thomas Aquinas phrased it; and it can do this because in it there is the reality of "the whole Christ" (*totus Christus*) as Thomas also said. In this the great Catholic doctor is at one with the great Reformer, Martin Luther. Calvin too saw this and in his treatise on the Lord's Supper he worked out a theological formulation which is singularly like some of the more recent writing on the subject coming from those on the Catholic side. By the work of the Holy Spirit, the faithful believer is taken into heaven where he is made a participant in the reality of Christ's life. We may not wish to talk about "heaven" in the almost spatial sense which doubtless Calvin had in mind; but the vital point is being made—that the life of the man who by faith has come to be "in Christ" is lifted to the plane of existence where the benefits of the Lord are available and where his presence is known in its risen splendour. Yet we must never forget that the "risen splendor" is of one who has died; hence the Eucharist is a celebration of death and resurrection, of divine presence and power in the midst of human suffering and anguish as well as human joy. In all this it is so powerfully expressive of the Christian position as a whole that we need not wonder at the central position which it has been given in the social process of Christian community through the ages.

We are now able to see also why the third way in which the Church manifests its continuity and identity is a consequence of the Word proclaimed and the sacrament that is celebrated. That third way is the life in grace or the life "in Christ" (as St. Paul taught us to think of it). The Lord's Supper is both the effective symbol of what that life is meant to be and also the means whereby men are empowered to enter into it. A life which has responded to God in Christ is a life which is lived with God in Christ. In other words, the communion or fellowship of the Christian with God through the remembered event, and the outward behavior which externalizes in the affairs of human society participation in that event, are tied up with the Eucharist because in both instances the same reality is effected: Jesus is made present still, in the heart and in the conduct of his faithful people.

We repeat that the "making present" is not simply a matter of human doing. The enduring Christian conviction is that the Holy Spirit, working with and in the human spirit, is the effective agent. In this book we have not had occasion to speak in any detail about the Holy Spirit. The omission is not quite as serious as some might think, however, since as someone has aptly remarked, the Holy Spirit's main interest is to point not to himself but to God in Christ and to work for the most part in an "anonymous" fashion without calling attention to his agency. Yet the work of the Spirit has been implied in all that has been said in our discussion of responsivity, the conforming of the various occasions in the creative advance to their intended aim, and the decisions which each entity makes as it positively elects the possibilities which are for its (and for the creation's) increasing growth in shared goodness or love. In the Eucharist, in particular, the Holy Spirit is the agent through whom God in Christ is known and by whom responding faith is possible for the reception of the present Lord and his achievement. Likewise in the life in grace, which is a life responsive to the act of God in the event of Christ, the Spirit is the enabling and empowering agency who awakens, deepens, strengthens, and accompanies all that is said, done, and thought.

A few pages back, the phrase of William Law about "the process of Christ" was quoted. The Christian is taken into that "process" by his entering into the event which was the concrete act of Jesus Christ himself, or of God in Jesus Christ. So the quality of human existence which was there manifested in a human life is reproduced in its measure in the believer. The primary mode of that reproduction is to be found in the communion of the believer with his Lord. Here he is identified for what he is, just as the Church which is his social setting as a Christian is identified for what it is by its enabling such relationship. External expression follows. The right order of things is naturally first the sharing in the Lord's risen life and then the action which makes manifest to others that the Christian has "been with Jesus." This right ordering means that Christian action has a purpose which makes it different in quality from an identical action performed by one who is untouched by the Christian faith. We are often shamed by those who "do the works" without having the inner fellowship; but we are permitted to believe that in such cases, of which there are so many, there is a hidden operation of God unknown to the truly good man who does not believe. Here is no Christian "imperialism" or arrogance but an insistence that God—the God whose way is always the way disclosed in Jesus Christ—is not confined to any boundaries which men may set up but can "get at" his children in ways past our finite understanding.

Remembering this, we must also say that action without some informing principle can be very "unprincipled action" and likely to prove to be "going about doing good" with inadequate motivation and inability to face difficulty. On the other hand, it is quite possible that a deeply felt relationship with God in Christ, lacking any outward channel of expression, will be sterile, and it may be a sign that the supposed relationship has not in fact been present at all. Some idol, perhaps doctrinal or perhaps practical, may have been substituted for the Lord.

It would be appropriate here to consider at some length the Christian conviction that the Lord is indeed "risen from the dead." However we shall postpone this discussion until the next chapter when the Resurrection will be taken as providing a crucial element in the Christian attitude to history. At this point it will be sufficient to remark that however we interpret the Resurrection, the basic reality in view for the Christian community is that all communion with and knowledge of God after the historical event of the life of Christ is in terms of and through the medium provided by that event as the activity of God in human existence, in a distinctive manner. This event, culminating (so far as visible evidence goes) in death, has about it what Whitehead once styled "the authority of supreme victory." That note was given by a series of experiences which convinced the first disciples that death had not put an end to Jesus nor halted the loving activity of God which he had disclosed. "He could not be holden of death," they said; and they regarded him as now triumphant over it. Thus the communion of the Christian with God is distinctive in that it is had in terms of that victory. The Jesus who is remembered in the Eucharist is the crucified and risen Lord; and the Jesus who is experienced in fellowship by the Christian believer is also the same living Lord, crucified and risen. As Dr. John Knox has so often reminded us, the Jesus who is "remembered" is the one who is a "living presence in the Spirit."

The internal relationship with the Lord is not to be conceived as a "looking back," but as a contemporary communion. Thus the inner Christian experience of discipleship is like the entire Christian understanding of how history becomes present. The reading of Scripture by the Christian is one way in which he knows this to be true, for there he is not discovering occurrences in the "dead past" but the living Lord of the present moment. In the Eucharist the remembrance is also the present reality of the originating event. And in the life in grace, the intimate sense of the relationship between Lord and disciple is no retrospective glance but a vital awareness of something going on here and now. The whole business hangs together, we might say.

We now turn to the second or external aspect of the life in grace. This is the behavior in action (of all sorts) of the Christian in the affairs of human society. Two points may be made about this aspect of discipleship. The first has to do with what is often called "the imitation of Christ"; the second with "rewards."

Christian action is indeed "the imitation of Christ"; but this should not be confused with "the imitation of Jesus." Many years ago an American author published a book called *In His Steps,* in which he attempted to show how that which Jesus said and did in his Palestinian career two thousand years ago could be reproduced in the then contemporary world. But the whole idea is a mistake. The Christian is not called to live, anachronistically, in Palestine during the first years of our era; nor can we envisage a trans-ference to our own time of the conditions which were then found. The "imitation" would be absurd; indeed it might very well turn out to be in dreadful contradiction to the spirit and intention of Jesus' own actions during his "days in the flesh." This sort of aping of another age is never a possibility. The poet has told us that "new occasions teach new duties"; a past age is never exactly repeated and the situation in which men find themselves today cannot be identical with that in which Jesus lived. But the other way of speaking, "the imitation of Christ," makes very good sense if by "Christ" we mean the living Spirit of Jesus as it speaks to men in our own time.

A very simple illustration will show my meaning. In Palestine in the first century it was doubtless the case that one could most effectively help a needy person by giving him an article of clothing or handing him a coin with which he could buy something he needed. Today we think that the consequence of this sort of assistance is much more likely to be damaging than helpful. We may succeed in "pauperizing" someone who needs to be assisted to stand on his own feet and who may very well require the help of agencies that are especially equipped in handling his problem. Of course there may be occasions when the coin will be needed. But there will be many more when concern for his need and an urgent desire to help him in meeting his difficulties will more effectively be expressed in other ways. A friend of mine always sees to it that a person who asks help is first of all given a good meal. Then he either takes him to a social agency or sees that he gets in touch with a caseworker who will aid him in finding a job, if he needs one, a place to sleep, and such medical or other assistance as may be needed. The Simon Community in Britain is a good case in point; it can do much more to help than individualistic charity—and so can the Good Samaritans and other agencies. Nor is this a matter of "cold comfort." As much personal interest and concern can be expressed in this way as in the older one. To avail oneself of such agencies and what they are able to do is to act in "imitation of Christ," although "imitation of Jesus" might indicate the less satisfactory procedure. The Spirit working in and released through Jesus in the days of his earthly existence and still communicated to those who turn to him in faith can teach us new duties to meet the new occasions.

It is quite probable that such an attitude will lead the contemporary Christian to cooperate with humanists, secularists, Communists, and others who do not "profess and call themselves Christian" but who are actively engaged in "doing the works" which in concrete actuality are the works of Christ. In the struggle for social justice, racial understanding, peace among nations, etc., in which the Christian surely must have his place, there may be very strange associations of different types. This does not diminish the importance of discipleship in more immediate if less obvious ways—in decency to one's neighbors and friends, loving relationships in one's home, refusal to nourish grudges or be angry because of criticism, and the effort to live in charity with one's associates. In such personal relationships or in the smaller groups in which men find themselves, there can be a very pertinent manifestation of the Christian identity. In these and other ways, as Luther wrote, the Christian is to be "an other Christ" to his neighbor. It is interesting that St. Benedict said almost exactly the same thing.

The second comment has to do with "reward." Here there has been much misunderstanding, usually in the direction of assuming that a Christian will act in the Spirit of Christ in order that he may receive some heavenly recompense after this life. I believe that this idea of recompense is alien to the life in Christ. The "I give that I may get" attitude is not only lamentable in itself but is very likely to produce a most unpleasant type of personality. It is also a demonstration that the basic factor in Christian discipleship has not been learned. I need hardly elaborate the point, save by recalling St. Francis of Assisi and his great prayer in which he spoke of not desiring "so much to be loved as to love" and put the whole calculus of "reward" in its proper place. The "reward" promised a Christian who acts in love is that he shall be able to share more love. The man who does God's good will because it will "pay" is hardly doing other than engaging in a speculation on the stockmarket!

In this connection it may also be observed that the genuinely Christian identity is manifested in an odd combination of spontaneity and determination. Acts and attitudes are not done so that others may "return the compliment." By their very nature they are spontaneous expressions of a loving care which is inescapable for one who has been grasped by love-in-action declared in the remembered event of Christ. On the other hand, determination (in sense of effort) is required, and in various ways. It is part of the response to such love-in-action to be informed about others, so that their situation may be understood. This is as much true of intimate personal relationships as of the bigger issues to which we have referred. It is also part of that responsive spirit to persist in caring, even when it seems a futile act on one's own part. When others may be prepared to give up because things are difficult, the Christian is to be persistent in his concern. He will never give up because he is "remembering," in the deep sense that I have continually urged, that in Jesus Christ there was Love which refused to be defeated by circumstance. This is "the Love that will not let me go," about which the hymn speaks.

The Christian is constantly driven back to his inner relationship with God in Christ, both for refreshment and for empowering. He is also brought to the Eucharist where he can receive the same refreshment and empowering; and to the Bible, where he sees vividly the Love which was in Christ Jesus. He is continually "renewed by the Spirit in the inner man"; his outward actions become a natural externalizing of his inner condition. Thus for him the historical event becomes a present fact of experience. The identity of the Christian community and its continuity with its origins are established in that fact-with-value proclaimed in the Word, celebrated in the sacrament, and exhibited in the life in grace of its members. So also for the member of the Church, establishment in his identity is by hearing the Word proclaimed (and where possible himself proclaiming it), by receiving the sacrament, and by inward and outward participation in the life in Christ.

CHAPTER 6

Miracle and History

There was a time when appeal was made consistently to the biblical stories of miracle as a proof that God was certainly at work in the events of Jewish history. More recently the stories of the Virginal Conception of Jesus and the Empty Tomb have been taken by some to be closely linked with the unique position which he is believed to occupy in the relationship between God and man. And in any event, the question of miracle is bound to be raised when we speak of the meaning of history in relation to Christian faith. Probably most of the readers of this book do not think that miracle proves anything about the place of Jesus in faith and constitutes, if anything, something of a problem. On the other hand, the patent fact that stories of miraculous occurrences are found in the Bible and especially in connection with Jesus Christ demands that we consider the subject.

Some years ago a correspondent wrote to protest to me about my having devoted space to this subject in a book on christology. He said that it was "rather antique modernism" to bother about the problem of what precisely miracle is commonly taken to mean and to consider afresh the significance of miracle in Christian faith. Neither historical nor critical study, on the one hand, nor philosophical enquiry, on the other, can resolve theological differences on this matter, he said; finally, one must accept miracle because it is an integral part of the historic faith or one must reject miracle and hence depart from that faith.

The other side of the issue was stated at about the same time by Dr. Derwyn R. G. Owen, Provost of Trinity College, Toronto, who wrote that "the apparent triumph of orthodoxy over liberalism in the last twenty years has tended to give the impression that many of the theological problems raised in the nineteenth century have been solved—science and religion, history and myth, natural law and miracle, Christianity and other religions." He went on to say that in his judgment "we are now beginning to realize that these problems were not solved but only shelved." It is interesting to note that Dr. Owen mentioned both miracle (in relation to natural law) and history (in relation to myth), but did not bring the two, miracle and history, together. In our discussion, we propose to do this.

Some defenders of the Christian faith still assume that what they style "the biblical view that God reveals himself through his acts in history" (a view to which, as has been seen, we have been subscribing) makes it unnecessary to consider what this view inevitably and logically demands: namely, that acts in history must be historically examined if they are to sustain the weight that is put upon them. They fail to see that because the Christian religion does originate in events in the realm of history, its representatives should engage in the most rigorous examination, not only of the evidence for miraculous occurrences (when they are part of the available record), but also of the concept of miracle itself, as well as of its relationship, negatively or positively, to the whole issue of the historical in Christian faith. They do not seem to understand that historical and critical study is itself part of the theological enterprise; nor do they see that the wider theological (and philosophical) issue cannot be avoided if any claim is being made about the truth of Christianity.

It appears to some of us that the problem of miracle has not been settled by movements in theology which were in the direction of more conservative positions. On the contrary one of the main defects of those movements has been the "shelving" of this and other issues, to use Dr. Owen's word. The way in which the questions were dealt with by devout Christian scholars in the preceding years may not have been satisfactory; but at least these scholars clearly saw the need for a new way of thinking about the meaning and place of the miraculous, even to the extent of urging that the word be given up because of its wrong associations and some substitute be provided which would not involve us in the vexing difficulties that the ancient term raises. Furthermore, some of those who reacted against this older "liberalism" would appear to have had a static view of the nature both of truth and of Christianity and a singularly literal-minded understanding of the historical assertions in the credal formulae which we have inherited.

Since this book is about Christian faith and history, we must focus attention on that aspect of the problem of miracle. But before we arrive at that point, we must say something about the scientific, philosophical, and wider theological aspects. These four, including history, are the areas in which discussion of miracle has particular relevance. First of all, however, we need a definition of the term miracle; and to that definition we must devote a few preliminary remarks.

The vulgar meaning of the word is probably this: a miracle is some event in the experience of men or in history which "violates" the regularities and consistencies of nature and historical sequence. But very few apologists would be prepared to accept this definition as satisfactory; they would not care to argue for the validity of the concept in those terms. A better definition would be along lines suggested by Professor A. E. Taylor in *The Faith of a Moralist.* This would see a miracle as an event which through its unusual character attracts attention but also awakens or deepens awareness of, faith in, and assurance of, the love of God. A question to which we must return is whether this sort of definition does not, in fact, so alter the common understanding that another word should be used in its place.

First, then, as to the scientific question. No instructed scientist today would deny that there is the possibility of the emergence of novelty in the world process. Nor, as a scientist, could he reject the possibility that such novelty may have the effect, upon those who are properly sensitive, of manifesting a focusing or concentration of the divine power and purpose in the created order. The world as it is now described by the scientist is not a uniformitarian world; it has variety, differences, heights and depths, "mores" and "lesses," novelties of many sorts. Nineteenth-century naturalism is no longer the necessary presupposition nor the inevitable consequence of scientific study.

On the other hand, science still requires, and this despite some recent writing which would in effect destroy the possibility of scientific research and experiment because of its implicit denial of any genuine consistency in the world of nature, the notion of what Dr. F. R. Tennant called "a relatively settled order," in which there is sufficient uniformity to make prediction possible and fruitful. This is another way of saying that science requires, and the world which science studies provides, sufficient faithfulness as to preclude unnatural or contranatural "violation" of the order of nature.

Second, as to philosophical considerations. The argument of this book has been for the acceptance of the conceptuality known as process thought. In that conceptuality (and indeed in any philosophy acceptable today) there is no *a priori* reason for denying, and every *a fortiori* reason for affirming, that the world is marked by just such variety and differences as science is unable to negate. In the famous phrase of A. S. Pringle-Pattison, it is marked by "continuity of process with the emergence of genuine novelty." This position is consistent with theism. On the other hand, the deistic view, in which God is taken to be remote from a world of which he is but the original creator, would demand the possibility of "intrusions" from without when things get "out of hand." But no sound case can be made for deism. Pantheism, in which nothing in particular manifests the divine because everything in general equally manifests it, is a view which no Christian is likely to accept; he cannot envisage God and the world as identical. But the panentheistic position, in which God and the world are interpenetrating but distinct one from the other, is in accordance with both scientific understanding and genuine

116

theism. God is immanent in the world, energizing through it at every point but energizing with varying intensity according to his purpose and also according to the possibilities presented to him in the creation. He is also transcendent, but not in the deistic sense. His transcendence is found in that he is both free in and also unexhausted by his immanent activity. In that case we shall expect a relative orderliness and consistency, which will be the reflection of the divine faithfulness in operation; but we shall also expect the apperance at different times and places of occasions or events in which the energizing activity of God in the world is more clearly, more intensively, and more concretely made manifest to us.

Third, as to theological matters. Christian theology has generally been intent on maintaining the two factors just noted: that God is faithful and consistent in operation, and that he also acts with greater vividness and intensity in certain moments and at certain places than at other moments or places. This is but another way of stating the main biblical witness, which insists on the freedom of God and the integrity of his purpose, as these were made known in his dealings with the people of Israel, while it also finds his activity particularly known in specific instances of those dealings upon which the biblical writers fix their attention.

Furthermore, in Christian theology it has been essential to preserve always the recognition of "the dearest freshness deep down things," to use Gerard Manley Hopkins' phrase. In the God-world and God-man relationship there are sufficient instances of newness, unexpected and unprecedented juxtapositions of event and apprehension, and the emergence of what is not contained in nor explained by earlier experience, to guarantee that "freshness"— the divine inexhaustibility of resource and concern. Christian experience indicates that in his concern for his human children God acts in such a fashion as to bring them, and the natural order as well, into a relationship which will secure for the whole creation, especially the human level, fullness of life to the degree that this is attainable in finitude.

Finally, in the theological area, Christian theology subsumes under the broad heading of divine providence both the regularities and the novelties. In his more general providence God is consistently and faithfully active in the whole creation, providing for it lines of development, averting the danger of anarchy and chaos, and patiently leading it to its goal. We may count on its relative orderliness. In his special providence God guarantees that to those who respond to him in faith, all things will be worked by him for their good. The "good end," to which St. Paul refers in Romans 8:28, is not ease of life nor deliverance from troubles and pain, but a relationship with God in the steady assurance that "nothing can separate us from the love of God," not even a Cross. In the end, the Cross becomes a way to provide just the fullness of life which God promises.

Now we may turn to the historical aspect. The evidence of the miraculous in the gospels and elsewhere in Scripture seems to indicate not so much "unnatural wonder" as relationship with God sustained through trial and trouble, giving grace and help, renewing faith, and deepening communion. Biblical form-criticism has enabled us to put the miraculous in a category subsidiary to the providential, as part of the care God exercises for his people, and as a way of understanding and describing the awareness of his presence as "infinite succor." It has made this possible for us because it shows the stories as part of the life of the Christian community, which sensed deeply its special relationship with God in the midst of his general providential care of his children. The miracles have their place as particular indications of that care, demonstrating divine favor, conveying divine strength, and disclosing divine concern—and all of this, not as contradicting God's way of working in the world, but as signal instances of that never-failing activity.

Examination of the material in the gospels which tells of miracle shows that their intention, as the story is told, is to demonstrate a working of God, not to emphasize its "unnatural" quality but to indicate vividly God's loving care, his ability to help his children, and his providential activity in the world. It is only when we import much later notions of fixity of natural law that we can read the material as if it were primarily intended to tell of "violations" of the regularity of nature or historical process. Concerning such things the biblical writers and editors had no knowledge, one way or the other, beyond the ordinary expectation of men that a certain orderliness marks the affairs of the world. Nor do the words used in the New Testament to speak of miracle imply any such set of ideas. *Dunamis* should be translated power or the release of power; *semeion* means sign of God's presence in action; and even *terrba* is best understood not so much as outright "marvel" as a striking and wonderful occurrence which receives attention: people sit up and take notice. We need not and we must not introduce later concepts into the rather naive material which we possess about the event of Chirst as reported to us in the New Testament—nor into the other contents of that book or of the Old Testament.

But we cannot excise the miraculous element, in this sense, from the gospels or the New Testament without damaging the integrity of the material as a true if "impressionistic" picture of Jesus as he was known to his disciples and preached in the primitive Christian community. On the other hand, we need not assume that the stories which have this miraculous quality are veridical in the sense that contemporary historical study might assume. Professor Bethune-Baker, in an essay written many years ago and included in the book *The Way of Modernism*, had some wise words to say on this point:

"I have no doubt that some of the stories in our gospels have their origin in the attempt to explain human experiences of an impressive and elusive kind by reference to powers and activities of a higher order than the known and natural. There was an established fashion in these matters, which still survives among those who have not become fully habituated to the fashion of thought which has gradually spread since Copernicus and Newton and Darwin"—and doubtless we should wish to add Freud and others—"and so the unknown quantity of which his contemporaries were aware in Jesus was accounted for by stories such as that of the Nativity; and some of his own experiences and their experiences in connection with him—the elusive quality of which ordinary measures could not cope with—experiences of which we should try to give a [psychological] account, were described in terms of events or occurrences of a wonderful character in the sphere of sense and sight and sound. To dismiss these stories as worthless, when we are seeking a true valuation of Jesus himself and the whole experience of which he was the centre, is to shut one's eyes to some of the bits of evidence we have about him and the impression he produced. It is not pitiful sophistry to use these stories as evidence of the kind I have indicated in making up our account of Jesus and the gospel history. They come to us . . . from the realm of poetry and picture; but experiences of men and women like ourselves underlies them, and so they help us to estimate the character and quality of that experience." However, Professor Bethune-Baker went on to say, "we cannot allow them to control our conception of God in the universe, or of the course of nature, or of the methods in which he is actually manifested in the cosmic process and human history."

When we consider the historical movement in the light of the process conceptuality, with its recognition both of continuity and novelty, with its insistence on openness to the future, and with its stress on the interrelationship of all events or occasions, we may well think that the concept of miracle requires expression in other words. If this is not done, there is the danger that others may be led to assume that we are still victim to the vulgar view of the miraculous as "violation" or "intrusion." It is my own belief that the word "providence" will serve us well in this particular connection.

During the 1940's, I had the privilege of editing some of the writings of Dr. William Porcher DuBose, the great and neglected American theologian of the earlier part of this century. Here is something that DuBose said, using the term "providence" in the inclusive sense which was suggested above and which here we are proposing: "God in natural things acts naturally and never contradicts himself or is inconsistent with himself. Insofar then as his providence is in and through natural things, there is no deviation . . . from what we call the 'causation' of nature"—and here I must interpolate the comment that the phrasing of DuBose at this point reflects an earlier and perhaps now rejected view of "natural cause," to which most of us would not today subscribe—"and yet, within the course of nature, if any Christian man will, as St. Paul says, love God and enter into the meaning and operation of his eternal and divine purpose, I know that he will find literally all things are working together, that God is working all things together, for his individual and particular good."

This notion may be extended to cover the whole issue of miracle. The basic point is that in the course of historical event certain particular events have a very special importance and value. This is what miracle really meant, I believe. If some think that this change misses something of the traditional Christian emphasis, I can only reply that in my judgment it is much more certainly a view which enhances and enriches our understanding of the love of God and his care for the children of men. After all, words matter less than the reality they seek to convey.

There are still some quarters—often fairly influential ones in certain Christian churches—where the credal words, "conceived by the Holy Ghost, born of Virgin Mary," are taken to be a plain statement of indubitable historical fact and hence in their literal meaning part of the Christian faith in Jesus Christ as incarnate Word of God. Some who adopt this position are contemptuous of biblical fundamentalism; but their own view is aptly styled "credal" fundamentalism. They do not maintain that the statement in the creed is true because it happens to be stated (as they think) in plain words of Scripture, but they believe it to be true because for them every phrase in the creeds which deals with historical happening must be accepted "in its straightforward meaning" by Christian believers. As we have already observed, there are others who would insist on the necessity for acceptance of this belief on the grounds that the Church has taught it or that the theological structure of Christianity, to their thinking, demands it.

It is obvious that such views cannot be accepted by the writer of this book. I have made clear, in earlier chapters, the way in which biblical critical study has affected our understanding of scriptural material. I have also argued for a quite different way of thinking about the teaching of the Church, especially in respect to its theological development. Furthermore, the approach to the past which has been urged in this book makes impossible any simple acceptance of narrative material (or any other type of material) which talks about events in the past. What then can we say about the virginal conception of Jesus Christ? More particularly, in view of our discussion of the larger issue of history and faith, concentrating in this chapter on reported miraculous events in the past and their significance in the historical perspective, what can we say about the significance, meaning, or value which Christians have found in the narratives that tell about the conception and birth of Jesus?

From the strictly historiological point of view, most New Testament scholars would agree that there is very little reliable data to which appeal may be made. Even Bishop Charles Gore was prepared to admit that much in the narrative found in the first two chapters of Matthew's gospel must be placed in the category of Jewish-Christian haggadah. This judgment, which applies most obviously to the Matthean story of the Magi and their visit to Bethlehem, applies equally to the first gospel's account of the birth of Jesus and the circumstances before and surrounding that birth. The other gospel account, in Luke's gospel, has an apparent historicity until we begin to analyze the style and patent intention of the narrative. It then becomes plain that the first two chapters, in which the account is found, are in a different class from the rest of the book. Their Greek style and idiom differs; they are evidently an addendum to the main body of the gospel. Many scholars think that they are early Christian folk tales, perhaps told among the christianized *am-ha-aretz* or simple people of the land. In this respect they are invaluable for their picture of naive Christian Jewish piety but hardly to be trusted for their factual value. It is also clear that the intention with which they have been used in the gospel itself is to indicate the special place and importance of Jesus as "sent by God," to be God's messenger, and to speak with divine authority. Hence they have an apologetic purpose, while they also show the beginnings of christological interpretation of the life of Christ, a point to which we shall return.

There is no other reference in the New Testament which an historian, working without presuppositions about the belief, would think asserted that Jesus was conceived by a virgin without human father. The efforts of such writers as J. Gresham Machen, G. H. Box, and Douglas Edwards, in books published long ago, to show the contrary seem to many of us remarkable for special pleading and for theological dictation of what the historical material ought to be telling us. It is difficult to see how anyone today can accept their conclusions as valid.

References in early non-canonical literature are hardly to the point here. The stories found in the apocryphal gospels are irrelevant since the Church itself rejected these as untrustworthy. The mentions which are made by other writers (St. Ignatius of Antioch, to name one) are plainly dependent on the gospels themselves and do not contain independent evidence. Later patristic writers and the Church's early tradition believed the stories, to be sure, but that hardly can be said to establish their original factual nature. Many a legend has found its way into the Christian tradition and has been piously accepted for a very long time.

There is no reasonable historical ground for maintaining the probability of the virginal conception. But we may be told that the grounds for maintaining it are not historical but theological.

123

Mention has been made of this view. But here we would seem to have reason to think that often enough a docetic tendency, which has dogged Christian belief and thought (and practice too, for that matter) through the centuries, plays an important role. It is said, for instance, that it would have been "unfitting" for the incarnate Son to have been conceived and born like other men and it would have been "fitting" that such an event as the Incarnation should have been accomplished in a very extraordinary way. Some simple people have even said that if God is Jesus' Father in a special sense, Jesus could not have had a human father! No responsible theologian would be likely so to confuse categories; but something of the same feeling may be discerned in those who speak so passionately of the peril of allowing human parentage on both sides to their Lord. To my own mind, one of the most damaging aspects of the case sometimes made for the virginal conception is the unconscious denigration of sexuality which is implied. This is sub-Christian or un-Christian; certainly it is unbiblical, for the Scriptures are witness to a healthy and accepting attitude to human sexuality as a gift of God which is sinful only when misused. Again, the insistence on the necessity for the virginal conception can rest on an implicit unwillingness to grant the full humanity of the Saviour. It is thought that he must be more God than man if he is to be in truth our Lord and our Redeemer. Such a view cuts at the very foundations of Christian faith, whose whole point is found in the reality of God's presence and act in the genuine and complete manhood of one who lived in this world of nature and event.

But very likely the main reason for the insistent emphasis on the virginal conception is that it is "part of a christology" (as one theologian has put it) that sees "the Eternal Word coming into the world rather than emerging out of it." Here the process conceptuality which we have adopted in this book is highly relevant to the subject. For the phrasing just quoted suggests a view of the relationship between God and the world which this conceptuality is concerned to deny and which in any event would appear to be damaging to genuine theism. What is more, in biblical thought God and the world are continually in closest interpenetrative relationship; while in the main stream of Christian theological development, God as the creative source acts continually in the created order through the agency of the Eternal Word, "by whom all things are made." God through the Word is present in and to every instant of creation, "upholding all things by the word of his power." He does not "come into" that creation, for he is always there—if he was not there, there would not be a world.

On the other hand, as we have insisted again and again, in any theology which takes a serious theistic line God is seen to act with greater intensity at one point or another, at one time or another. His purpose leads him to focus his activity at this rather than at that place, in this rather than in that life, in order to accomplish the ends which his love has in view.

Now the Christian faith makes the claim that in the historic human life of Jesus Christ we find the center of the divine activity through the Word in the realm of happening or event. That is part of the meaning intended when Christianity is called an historical religion. But Christ need not be seen as a divine intervention, as it were from outside. But then what could we conceivably mean by such an "outside" from which intervention was made? Rather, he is the fullness of the Word's action in human affairs, in the concrete reality of a human life. Preparation for that fullness went on long before the event of Christ. The consequences of that fullness we share, "grace heaped upon grace." Unless we allow ourselves to be bewitched by spatial imagery, which we take as if it were literal fact and not as a way in which the value, importance, and significance of the event were indicated by those to whom it had meaning, we can just as well say that the Eternal Word "emerged in fullness, humanly speaking, in Jesus," as that the Eternal Word "came down from heaven." For heaven is not literally "up" and the earth literally "down"; these are words which can be used with high symbolic purpose but they should be taken with imagination, for we are not describing in them some "descent" from outer-space to this planet.

Certainly the Christian would not think that the divine operation in and through the Man Jesus—and this is what we are getting at when we speak of the Word of God incarnate in him—is identical with that operation elsewhere. In the Johannine word, Jesus is *monogenes*—"unique." In him there is supreme "novelty" in the midst of a continuity of God-man and God-world relations. But the novelty is not in contradiction to the universality of the divine activity in nature and history. To use von Hügel's fine phrase, it is "the implied goal and center" of that activity. To say that Jesus Christ is "incarnate Word of God" is to say that he is that one in whom the self-expressive act of God was focused "for us men and for our salvation"; and the practical consequence of such faith is the "life of Christ" of which we have spoken, for in him God is manifest in our humanity as "the way, the truth, and the life" for men.

When the word "unique" is used of Jesus Christ, we need to be very careful. The term can suggest an event utterly without parallel, without preceding intimation, and simply anomalous in our experience. It can also mean what Professor C. F. D. Moule has suggestively styled "uniqueness of inclusion," in which in one special moment or occurrence there is a vivid concentration of what hitherto and elsewhere has been intimated, hinted at, dimly perceived and known, vaguely revealed and accepted. My contention is that only in the second sense is the word appropriate for Jesus.

What shall we say about the stories of the virginal conception? Are they not an imaginative and poetic way of stating precisely this significance which Christians discover in Jesus? Are they not a way of asserting the value which has been found in the fact? The idiom used is mythological, if you will; clearly it is more like poetry than dull prose. But "Emmanuel, God with us" is what the stories are saying. The account is given with beauty and it evokes wonder. The stories may seem like a fairy-tale; but the tale is told about the historic and risen Lord whom Christians worship and would serve and of whose historicity the Church stands continually as witness. Here is poetic truth which can be much more true than simple literal prose, although its manner of being true is different from such prose. If one uses the word miracle to signify a compelling happening which human minds cannot completely understand and describe and which speaks to us of God and his purposes, then every birth is rightly described as a miracle—for those who have the eyes of faith to see God's part in human procreation. Above all, however, the birth of him who for Christian faith is the incarnate Word, Lord, Master, and Savior, is in that sense a miracle. But in the vulgar sense, in which miracle means unnatural or contranatural occurrence, it is not a miracle at all. To think of it as such is to deny a sound historical view. Some of us feel that to speak of the conception of Christ in that sense is to deny the real meaning of the Incarnation, to introduce biological absurdity at the heart of our religion, and to make the figure of Jesus Christ alien from those whom he was willing to call his brethren. Above all, it is to confuse the abiding importance and value of the historical event in the past with the temporary thought-forms of an earlier age and by doing so to make the possibility of faith difficult if not impossible for our contemporaries.

At the very heart of Christian faith is the conviction that Jesus Christ is "risen from the dead." By what the New Testament calls "the mighty act of God," the Jesus who had companied with his disciples in Palestine, preaching the Kingdom of God, healing the sick, impressing those who met him by his commanding presence and his spiritual authority, was triumphant over death; and of this victory the first Christian believers declared they had been assured by "many infallible signs." This same declaration, accompanied by this same assurance, is still made by the fellowship of Christian believers. It is one of the chief marks of the identity of the Christian community and its continuity with its past. The Christian Church does not concern itself with a dead hero of some two thousand years ago but with One who is known as living and regnant Lord.

The earliest evidence for belief in the Resurrection is found in St. Paul's First Letter to the Corinthians, where in the fifteenth chapter the Apostle gives his converts the tradition "which he had received." Jesus Christ had indeed been crucified; he had died on the Cross; he had been buried in a grave. But he had been "seen by" or had "appeared to"—the Greek verb permits of either translation—a number of his disciples, beginning with St. Peter and ending, so far as St. Paul's listing goes, with St. Paul himself, who since he had not been a member of the disciples' band and yet had "seen the Lord" described himself "as one born abortively." The whole of the New Testament pulses with the conviction which is stated in this passage. The first Christian communities were overwhelmingly possessed by the certainty that Jesus the Messiah was "raised from among the dead" and was now in present and immediate contact with his people through the Spirit.

The accounts of the Resurrection in the closing chapters of the four gospels were written down long after the event, long after St. Paul's words in I Corinthians, and long after the primitive Christian fellowship had been caught up in the faith in the risen Lord. For the historical scholar, these accounts show obvious signs of Christian theological and apologetical interest; they can hardly be accepted as reports by eye-witnesses. This is not the place to make an extended study of the narratives in order to demonstrate the christological and apologetical intention which patently governs them. Such a study has been made by many experts in the field of New Testament research and their conclusions are readily available. Most recently an admirable summary of this work, with an attempt to deal with its conclusions and their significance, has been written by C. F. Evans, *The Resurrection of Christ.* With very few exceptions, these experts, continental, British, and American, recognize at the least the historical dubiety of the empty tomb sections of the gospel material and find the main weight of evidence in the stories of the "appearances" of Jesus and in the witness to the disciples' certainty of his vindication by God.

What matters here is not the precise historicity, in the factual sense, of the evangelical accounts but the significance of the primitive Christian conviction of Jesus' rising "from among the dead." Indeed, it is impossible to make any genuinely satisfactory reconstruction from the various accounts of the experiences which led to the Christian conviction, since the material which is at our disposal is confused and confusing both in the purported occurrences and in their chronology. But once we have adopted the view of history for which this book has argued, especially (in the present context) with respect to the way in which information about past event is conveyed to us through a living community of faith, the point does not rest in the precise historicity of the narratives but in the shattering faith of which they all speak. This faith was not made up out of nothing but rested upon the conviction, to which all the material bears witness, that men were delivered from fears and anxieties and found newness of life in the experienced reality of a presence and power which was of and from the Lord himself. Thus we today need not be frightened if the reports are confused and confusing; we are free to concern ourselves with what really matters and what they are intent on asserting. This is the proclamation that Jesus Christ is not "dead and out of the way," nor is he merely an "immortal spirit"; but that through some means, the details of which we do not know, he so "energized" (to use the Pauline word) in his disciples, beginning with St. Peter, that they knew with a certainty born of deepest experience that their Master was "alive" in the fullness of his personal existence. In consequence they were sure that he was to be with them "to the end of the world."

When we put our stress here, we can regard with equanimity the various differing conclusions, whatever they may be, concerning the details of historical event, since we realize that the full Christian assurance is dependent upon the undeniable historical fact of a conviction which is written over the whole New Testament and verified in the continuing experience of faithful Christians through the ages down to our own day.

What is included in this conviction?

First of all, that Jesus is truly alive not only in the divinity which Christians ascribe to him when they speak of the activity of God in his human existence, but in the full integrity of his person. As traditional theology has put it, his "human nature" is still united with the eternal Word who in him "was made flesh and dwelt among us." The Christian faith asserts that in Jesus the Word—Deity in his self-expressive activity—so possessed and energized through a full, genuine, and free human life, that the divine action and the human response were truly a unity. He was "raised from the dead" in the totality and integrity of his person, with "all things appertaining to the perfection of man's nature" (as Article IV of the Anglican XXXIX Articles phrases it).

Thus, he is the center and focus of the divine-human relationship, not alone in "the days of his flesh," but for ever, since in him that relationship is clinched and established for what it truly is intended to be. The Word of God is indeed always the ground of human life, since he is both the undergirding reality in the entire creation and also pre-eminently at work in human nature; but this relationship is in Jesus brought to climatic completion. Hence Jesus Christ risen from the dead is the way in which henceforth men most directly and immediately may come to the reality of God. The Epistle to the Hebrews puts this in its memorable phrase about Christ's being "the new and living way through the veil" to the center of heaven itself.

Secondly, this carries with it an important corollary, not always adequately recognized in Christian thought. The corollary is one which to those who have followed the argument of this book will be obvious. History, the realm of event, makes a difference to the God-man relationship. The event of Christ, whose "uniqueness" (if we still wish to use this word) is both the speciality of every other event in being singular and unrepeatable and also the particularity of the action achieved in him, has changed the relationship between God and man. If every occurrence in nature and history has the effect of altering the situation thereafter, as we have argued must be taken as a simple fact to be accepted, then the at-one-ment of God and man wrought out in Christ has established a new situation in a peculiarly important way—the utter vividness of God's action there, coupled with the utter adequacy of the human response, means that for ever afterward men live in the light of the achievement.

This works both ways. It means that through the solidarity of our human existence, in which we are all "members one of another," what was done in Christ has its application and significance for every man. But it also means that on God's side, the event has done more than merely manifest what has always been the case. It has done that, to be sure; but in doing it, the new expression of divine concern has brought about, in and for God, a new mode of relationship which (apart from that event) would not have been realized. This is why the Christian mission, as F. D. Maurice rightly saw, is to labor to make men aware of what has happened and what henceforward is the case, urging them to accept what has been accomplished and thus to enter into their inheritance as participants in the achievement wrought out by God in Christ.

Furthermore, Christian faith in the light of the conviction of Christ's victory over death, has seen that precisely because he is risen from the dead and is now central to the whole God-man relationship, the results and effects of his deed have a backward as well as a forward significance. The Abelardian view that the principal way of at-one-ment is the awakening of loving and obedient response to the care of God manifest in the event of Christ, must be associated with an equally strong insistence that the love of God, there manifested and operative, has changed the way things are and the way things go. Hence all men everywhere, before and after and apart from the knowledge of the historic Jesus, are seen by God and related to him in that context. God has "nowhere left himself without witness" and he is the same God who is always faithful and loving. Yet acting with an intensity that has made a difference and self-expressed through Jesus with a peculiar intimacy and directness, he now is always working, often in subtle and mysterious ways, to accomplish for all men, before or after the dated event of Christ, that which once for all he did in Christ.

In the third place, the Resurrection of Christ from among the dead is the guarantee that human nature and human experience count with God. The theological way of stating this is to affirm that the Resurrection cannot be separated from the Cross which in temporal successiveness came before nor from the Ascension and "Session" which in temporal successiveness came after. The Jesus who was "raised" is the same Jesus who as a man suffered death upon the Cross and who now is enthroned in full human nature at the right hand of God as King of men and Lord of their lives. Put less metaphorically, the Resurrection demonstrates that while it is of the very nature of God to participate in the experience of men, since he is both their creative ground and the underlying activity in preserving them in existence, he has so wrought in Christ that humanity and human experience are now known to him and shared by him with a fullness that otherwise is unprecedented. This knowing and sharing by God were not for a brief time only; they continue as "remembered" forever in the consequent nature of God—God as affected by the world. This is what it means to say that historical happening makes a difference in the God-man relationship. God, who is unsurpassed by anything not himself, has yet surpassed himself in the act of Christ because he has been provided (in response to his own prevenient activity) with a possibility of working that otherwise was not his. Simply, God now includes what the human existence and achievement of Jesus was and did.

Fourth, the Resurrection of Christ gives the assurance that

132

death in at least one sense does not write *finis* to the significance of human life. There may or there may not be what the Greeks and others have called immortality. But the Christian conviction, "the promise of faith," is that God who creates and constitutes human nature in the first place and most patiently and caringly guides and saves it during the span of our mortal existence, also can and will reconstitute and re-create that nature by "resurrection from the dead." This affirmation has nothing to do with the chemistry of the human body; it is not concerned with the flesh and blood which St. Paul told us "cannot inherit the kingdom of God." It has to do with us as living routings of event or occurrence or occasions, with us as men in the solidarity of our humanity and in our belonging together. The Resurrection of Christ tells us that our resurrection is the act of God whereby he accepts what we have done "in the flesh" and makes this count for him in the divine plan as it has counted in our own experience. The mode in which that takes place is not known to us; at the very least, however, it signifies of us what *a fortiori* it has signified of Jesus himself: that we are received in some appropriate and possible fashion into the life of God, with our human brethren, to affect God himself—he rejoices in our triumphs, he suffers in our anguish, he is ready to employ our achievements for the furthering of his own ends of love. The "communion of saints" in the life of God is a way of speaking of this abiding truth. Hence we can see that it is we ourselves, as it was Jesus himself, who are raised to the divine acceptance and employment. Our history has counted.

This brings us to a fifth point. I have just written "are raised," not "will be raised." This phrasing is demanded because the resurrection of us men is not simply an event toward which we look forward; it is a present reality. St. Paul is constant in this emphasis; the Johannine literature says the same when it speaks of "eternal life" which now is offered to men, not held out to them for future reception. By our sharing here and now, in the Christian community of faith which continually brings the event of Christ's Resurrection into contemporary relevance through the working of the Holy Spirit, in Christ's already risen life in God and for the world, we whose life he shared are "risen with him." The whole of Christian life, thereafter, is the implementation of that which is thus already accomplished. Because we are risen with him, St. Paul tells us, we are "to seek those things which are above." We are to act now as being what already in Christ we are. At our physical death or at such time as we are more perfectly fitted, the "new being in Christ" will take over the whole of our lives and thereby bring to rich fulfillment and fruition that which already is present in "earnest." History moves in us toward this subjective aim.

Finally, faith in the Resurrection includes more than human life and more than the realm of human affairs. It is a symbol of the confidence that the whole created order, in which God creatively energizes, will also share in the divine realization of good. How other rational beings, if there are any such elsewhere in the universe, can be brought thus to share in God's reign or kingdom we are ignorant. We could not know. How the material stuff of things, the created fabric of the universe, will make its contribution to God's abiding triumphant kingdom, we do not know. We could not know, certainly at this stage of human knowledge. But to believe that God will be, and in principle although not in its working out already is, victorious over sin, evil, and death, wherever these are to be found, and that his kingdom and royal rule in love shall have no end, is the legitimate and necessary extension of our faith in what has already been accomplished in Christ who is "risen from among the dead." Thus, to return again to our main interest, history and nature are knit together in a single movement toward a divinely intended goal. In Tennyson's words, "The whole round world is every way knit by gold chains about the feet of God."

CHAPTER 7

The Fulfillment of History in God

The concluding words of the preceding chapter bring us directly to a consideration of the way in which history finds its fulfillment in God, the topic to which this final chapter will be devoted.

This book has been a study of the relation between history and the Christian faith. The study demanded that we analyze some of the meanings of the word "history." It required a consideration of the historical quality of the Bible since within the Christian community the Bible serves as the recording of the events in the past which the Church regards as necessary and central to its life. It also necessitated some examination of the ways in which the identity of the Christian fellowship and its continuity with its own past have been maintained and expressed. Finally, because in so much traditional discussion of the value of history for faith, miracle has played a very central role, we devoted one chapter to that subject, with special attention to the material which tells of the virginal conception of Jesus and his rising from the dead.

The reader will have recognized that this book has been written by one who is a believing and practicing Christian. This has not made impossible a relatively objective examination of the material under discussion, however. Everybody has some stance which he adopts as he thinks and talks about a subject. Once this has been admitted, others can take it into account and make the necessary allowances. The one thing not possible is *the sort* of claim to objectivity which pretends that it works with no beliefs, no presuppositions, no broad assumptions. That is all too likely to lead to the gravest error, because it brings with it no criticism of ideas; in my judgment the claim to such complete objectivity is both pretentious and absurd. But although I am a Christian I have become more and more convinced over the years that the traditional statement of Christian faith, so long accepted in the churches, is in need of radical revision—perhaps better said, radical reconception. In making some slight contribution to this task, I have adopted the conceptuality called process thought as the most satisfactory of possibilities available to us today; and in several books I have tried to look at different Christian beliefs in the light of that conceptuality. Nor am I alone in this, since in the United States for almost half a century, theologians of different denominations have been working along these lines, while now in Britain, and elsewhere, the recognition of the significance of this conceptuality has been recognized, at long last, and some younger men have got to work on the job of reconsidering familiar Christian assertions in this new light.

Nowhere does process thought serve us so well as in a treatment of the subject of this concluding chapter. Fulfillment in God—whatever can this mean? In what sense can we talk meaningfully of history as having its end in God? In a world of energy-events, where facts are given with value or importance, where dynamic movement is the basic pattern, and where social relationships mark every instance of creation, can there be any other goal than the on-going process itself? That we must say that history is fulfilled in God seems to me a requirement of Christian faith. But how can we say it? That we must say it in terms of a process conceptuality is to me equally obvious. But is this possible? The intention of this chapter is to show that we can say it, with certain modifications of conventional ideas, and that the process way of thinking helps us in the saying.

In another book (*The Last Things in a Process Perspective*), I have attempted to show that the traditional four—death, judgment, heaven, and hell—could be given a new interpretation, but their basic significance retained, by placing them in the context of the process conceptuality. In that book I urged that the fact of human death, the fact of appraisal of the achievement of each human life and of society as a whole, the facts of maximal realization of possibility or the anguish of failure in realization, are not only part of the total Christian way of seeing human existence but are given in concrete human experience. There is a fit here between such experience as men know in the depths of their self-existence and the implications of the Christian proclamation of God's love to his weak and sinful children. Now I wish to urge that the fulfillment of the movement of historical event, which inevitably includes within it particular incidents including also the sons of men, is an integral part of Christian belief and is also given in human awareness of the sense of existence. That entails the assertion that the entire process of creative advance, in its particular expressions during the on-going movement and in its comprehensive point, is neither aimless nor futile but finds its completion in acceptance by God. This affirmation provides the starting point in our present discussion.

In the process conceptuality which we have adopted, the divine reality is seen as "dipolar" in character, to use Professor Charles Hartshorne's term. That word requires explanation. God is not only the unoriginate source of potentiality who is active as the principle of concretion in granting the initial aim or vocation for each occasion or entity in the creation; he is also the recipient of all that is achieved in that creation, taking into himself, accepting for what it is, and using for further activity back in the creation the ways in which each entity or occasion has decided for its own realization, contributed to others, and aided in the general purpose of good. In Whitehead's words, God is both "primordial" and "consequent." The dipolar conception is an assertion that in one aspect, abstractly and taken apart from relationship with the world, God may be described as eternal or timeless and absolute; but in another aspect, concretely and in relationship with the world, he is everlasting (inclusive of and participant in the time series but in his own eminent way) and relative or related. The difficulty with what Hartshorne styles "classical theism" is that it has consistently taken the former or abstract aspect as the defining characteristic of God, thus suggesting a static and unrelated deity rather than the active and loving God of Christian faith. In process conceptuality, this is reversed. It is the latter, everlasting and related and concrete aspect which is the more inclusive. That is how God is; the other aspect is purely formal or structural.

When God is taken to be self-contained and self-sufficient, entirely "from himself" without any relationships upon which he may be said in a real sense to count and even "depend," it is hard to talk meaningfully about the temporal succession of events in a world of process making any contribution to him and having any fulfillment for him which is not a denial of their freedom and intrinsic significance. But when the concreteness of God in relationship is given central place, with God's actuality in his unfailing and faithful relationship with creation, then what goes on in the world can be seen as really important, not only in itself but for God.

In such a conceptuality "becoming" is able to include "being," rather than the other way around. The usual list of divine attributes—such as eternity, infinity, omnipotence, omniscience, ominpresence, wisdom, righteousness, and the like—have an adverbial value, describing how God is and functions in one or other of his aspects. Thus God is always related, infinitely loving, aware of all actualities as actual and of all potentialities as potential, possessed of the only true power which is the capacity to love without fail and to act indefatigably in love, everywhere operative through his love for his creatures. He cannot be surpassed by anything other than himself, since by definition he is the unsurpassable one who is worshipped; yet he is able to increase, augment, and enrich himself through his relationship with the creation where he is at work. Furthermore, he is able to use the achievements of the creaturely events for further and richer expression of his goodness or love—which is to say, of himself, in the on-going creative advance which is the cosmic process.

God is unique in that he persists through all perishing, whereas the events or occasions in the process of creation perish when they have achieved their satisfaction through fulfilling their aim or purpose. He is also unique in that he alone is worthy of worship because he is supremely good or excellent. Yet he is not the "exception," in Whitehead's word, to all the principles required to make sense of the world; he is their "chief exemplification," although in an eminent or full sense. Whitehead's point here is often misinterpreted; it is thought that he meant that God is one instance of those principles and in no sense "exceptional." But Whitehead did not say that; nor does a careful reading of the last pages of his Gifford lectures *Process and Reality* make such a view possible. On the contrary, God is different from other entities in respect to his supremacy, his functioning as the "ultimate irrationality" or chief explanation who cannot be "explained" but must be accepted as the necessity for explanation, his persisting through all process. By that very token he is the eminent instance, as we have said, of the principles which he does exemplify among the categories required to make sense of the world.

In this conceptuality we have another mode of metaphysical discourse; it provides another vision of reality. Metaphysically it proceeds from lived experience, observed and known and intuited. This means that such a felt moment is taken to be important and indicative as a clue to how things go. Generalizations are then made and these are applied as far as possible and to as much as possible. If a generalization works or fits, making sense of things, it provides a vision which is trustworthy but by no means absolutely true. The vision is subject to correction; but as long as it serves its purpose it provides a way of seeing things and a way of acting as human beings. It offers an answer to the human question about how things are and go, so far as the human mind can grasp the what and the how of the process of which it is a part.

This long presentation of the process conceptuality has filled out the earlier discussion at the beginning of this book. But its special purpose here has been to prepare the reader for the following assertion: God, conceived in this way, shares in the initiated events (which he himself has provided with their aim), he works to bring potentiality into actuality, and he fulfills himself in realizing the goal which is his. That goal is the widest sharing in love which includes the realization of the events of which the world is made up. It is God who provides the vocation necessary for each energy-event, who lures entities toward the making of the right decisions for their proper fulfillment, and who receives into himself that which has been accomplished or achieved through those decisions as they have led to the fulfillment of each energy-event, each routing of occasions, each component of the process. Thus, as we have said before, he is both the chief (not the only) causative agent and he is the final affect in the creative advance.

We have now arrived at the place where we may speak meaningfully of the fulfillment of history in God. The best way to get at this, we shall find, is through consideration of a further point stressed in process conceptuality: "objective immortality."

Let us suppose that a good man has lived his seventy years, doing his work, living happily with his wife and raising a family, knowing and helping many friends, and in the course of those years and through those experiences making his personality. He dies, as do all men. The funeral is held, his body is cremated, the ashes are placed in a small box, and the box is sealed in a receptacle which is deposited in an appropriate resting place. On the receptacle is engraved a memorial which reads, "John Jones, Born 1899, Died 1970." Underneath these words are some others: "Beloved Husband of Mary Louise and Father of John, Jr., Anthony, and Frances." The years pass. His wife will die; his children will marry and have their sons and daughters and they too will all die. In the office in which he worked, John Jones's very existence will be forgotten. What is more, since John Jones was not a notable statesman or a famous writer or a distinguished scientist, he will not be remembered at all, after the passage of a few years.

Is this, then, the end of it all? Is John Jones and everything that he did or failed to do, loved or disliked, accomplished, felt, and thought, entirely finished? Is it a case of over and done with? Looking at the matter without introducing any religious convictions we may have, what did it all come to? Did the happening—for in the process conceptuality the life of John Jones is a happening or series of happenings taking a specific direction or route—make any difference, anywhere, to anything, to anybody?

Now this question which we ask about John Jones is a question we must also ask about any event or occasion in the cosmic process, about any series of occasions, and about the process itself insofar as it consists of its several (nearly infinite number of) happenings. And since the process is composed of events which are both in continuity with others and yet have an element of novelty or freshness—in other words, since the process is an historical process in the sense that it is made up of facts with value—we must ask whether that process in its totality has made any difference? Has it counted? And if so, for what or whom?

Again, since every event has achieved its own satisfaction in some way, for good or ill and with whatever degree of adequacy in the realization of its aim, we must inquire whether or not the richly complex, interrelated society of such occasions (each of them a focus) can be said to have achieved some fulfillment. Or put in another way, in what sense and in what way is the historical movement valuable, significant, meaningful, and really (not superficially) important? Has it made a worthwhile contribution, useful to the divine reality that is both its chief cause and its final affect?

The answer to these questions is suggested by the two last words of the last paragraph: "final affect." This is where objective immortality comes into the picture. We have already cited Whitehead's answer to his student Ferrè that reality is to be characterized in this way: "It matters; and it has consequences." Matters to whom or to what? Has consequences for what or for whom? Obviously to a considerable extent for the other creaturely entities in the process which are moving toward the actualizing of their aims, in whatever manner and degree. Obviously for the on-going itself, since that is dependent for what will happen upon the decisions which have been made in the past and are being made in the present and hence determine what that future is going to be. But beyond that?

The response which a process theologian must make is that reality, by which I assume both Ferrè and Whitehead intended to denote the on-going of occasions or energy-events, matters and has consequences for God and in God. This is bound to be the case if God is truly the final affect, the ultimate recipient of that which is achieved or accomplished. Then the fulfillment of history in its deepest sense (which will include nature understood historically as well as the realm of human events) is not only within itself, so to say, so far as that takes place. It is also and more importantly in God. God takes into himself and treasures the occasions one by one. He does the same with the series of occasions; and likewise he receives and values the total process of history itself for what it has done. Having thus received it, he lovingly uses it in ways that are harmonious with, and for the further implementation of, his own aim—which is nothing other than the expression of love in the creation as it moves forward beyond that point. In a word, history is made up of what matters; and it has consequences not only for itself but for God in what we have called his "consequent" nature.

To talk in this way is to run counter to a long and well-established tradition of philosophical theology. The view which for centuries has prevailed is that God is the first but that he is not the last. He starts the creation but he does not "get anything out of it" which ultimately matters, since the creation can make no genuine contribution to him. This widely accepted view is tied in with the conception of God to which we have referred: that he is so much the self-contained and self-sufficient "first cause," "unmoved mover," and "absolute being" that already, before there is a creation at all, he has everything because already he is everything. It is my belief, shared by all who accept the process view, that this view is false, however hallowed by centuries of philosophical and theological thought.

What is worse, it is (in my judgment) *viciously* false since its effect is to deprive the creation of any real significance. History cannot have any enduring meaning on those terms. Yet we have insisted that wherever men encounter event they insist on there being value or importance there, incarnate in the fact. And the only way in which any entity can be said to have such value, in a genuine sense, is by seeing it as able to contribute not only to its fellow-creatures but to whatever or whoever is the divine agency in, through, and with the process of which they are a part. If everything that I say or do is already contained within the divine being for whom "consequences" cannot ultimately count or make a difference, then whatever I say or do is irrelevant in the long run. It may have an immediate and proximate importance, for me or for my friends or for the period in which I live, perhaps for the brief future; but in the long run and ultimately it does not "matter."

On the other hand, granted the perspective we have been urging, with its recognition of God's "consequent" nature as the concrete actuality with which we reckon, then what I say or do does matter; it matters to God and it has consequences for and (we dare to say) in God. The practical effect of this assurance is that I am able to see in my saying and doing an importance, greater than the obvious and visible ones. What I do or say changes the pattern of the process of which I am part and provides for the enduring and supreme God both a possible enrichment of his relationship with the world or (tragically) a possible suffering through his having to reject or "negatively prehend" that done by me which cannot be accepted by him because it cannot be harmonized with his loving purposes. The sense of being able to make a worthwhile contribution, and the sadness at not having made one, together bring me to a renewed and vivid responsibility.

I realize that what has been said requires a radical readjustment in the thinking of most of us who have been brought up on the older view. Certainly it meant such a readjustment for me when I began to think through the implications of the conceptuality I had been led to accept because it seemed to me sound and right. On the other hand, I believe that while many have never thought of formulating the matter in this way, we actually live on the assumption that the situation is as I have tried to describe it. The ordinary believing Christian would perhaps regard it as blasphemous to think or say that what he does through his decisions in a world of historical event makes a contribution to God. Yet he acts on that basis, exactly to the degree that he is a faithful Christian. He believes that "there is joy in heaven over one sinner that repenteth." He believes that in a serious sense his desire to live in a way "pleasing to God," and to obey what he takes to be God's will for him, matter to God, while his refusal to live in a way thus "pleasing to God" and his making self-regarding and self-destructive decisions is a disappointment to God. He wants never to bring sorrow to God. I remember an old priest saying to me, many years ago, "Every sin is a wound inflicted on the merciful heart of God." This is exactly the point. In all these ways, the faithful Christian is assuming that what he does matters and has consequences and that this is not only in respect to the world of creaturely happenings but to God himself.

One of the useful terms employed in process thinking is "the divine memory." Memory, as we know, is the presence in our minds of that which has occurred in the past. We have already noted another way in which the word may be used, when we have spoken of how the Christian proclamation of the Word, celebration of the sacrament, and life in grace are a "remembering" of the event of Christ. But God also remembers. We may and must say that; and I believe that the frequent use in the Old Testament of phrases about God's "remembering" or about the prayer of his people that he will "remember them" for good, is very relevant here.

Of course the word "memory" and its cognates can suggest simply a "looking back." Or they can be taken to mean, as a friend once put it in criticism of the view I am here advancing, that God "plays over and over again a motion picture film made of my life or of other happenings in the world." But such a conception of memory seems to me very superficial. There is a much deeper meaning of memory; and I have found no better expression of it than in some words written recently by my friend David Edwards in his book *The Last Things Now*. I quote these words here, without intending to identify Mr. Edwards with the position I have taken, from which I know he would dissociate himself in large measure:

"Every man is aware of the importance of memories in his life. . . . His memories make up much of what makes a man; they record the events which constitute the pattern into which new events are fitted and become personal for him. In every man's experience of his own past may be found a hint of what the union of God with his creatures may mean eternally. God is before any creature was . . . but the taking of God's creation into eternal life enriches him. . . . From our own experience of our memories we can go on to glimpse God's will and capacity to remember for ever the whole of creation, each moment of life in it, so that the life of God completely counteracts what the philosopher A. N. Whitehead used to call 'the perishing of occasions.' And more: since God loves people and things . . . he remembers completely that person or that thing as a person or thing that was shaped in the whole of life before death. But even here the comparison of the human and divine memories cannot be ended. When we remember, the person remembered can 'come alive,' as we say, for a moment of illusion. A period of history can be 'recreated' in a book of history. And this, the most impressive aspect of the power of our memories and the summit of all historical work, can be a clue to the will of God to remain the

God of Abraham, Isaac, and Jacob, and the God of every living creature, rescuing all that has existed from the 'hell' of eternal death."

Mr. Edwards then goes on to cite a series of biblical passages which bear on the matter: Psalm 20:3, Psalm 132:1, Psalm 25:7, all of which speak of God's "remembering," and he concludes with the prayer of the penitent thief to Jesus on the Cross: "Remember me when you come to your throne" (Luke 23:43).

I should not accept all of the phraseology here, but I believe that Mr. Edwards has made his point. Essentially that point is that memory can be "living" memory, in which the "objective immortality" of what has happened in the realm of historical event indeed "comes alive" in God in his "consequent" nature—and having thus come alive, is never lost. History thus finds its true fulfillment in God's own life; and because God is the abiding one, what is fulfilled in him because it has been made alive in him is fulfilled in such a manner that it is determinative, in its measure, of the "contents" of the divine life. It enriches it or improverishes it, if we may dare to say the latter; it makes our human accountability a most serious matter; and it provides God with opportunity for further advance, or denies him this opportunity, in the whole process of creative advance.

In his *The Living God and the Modern World*, Peter Hamilton has written a sentence that sums up all this: "Everything of any value [is] immortalized in his [God's] supremely personal life." To be "immortalized" in God's life is to find fulfillment, such as can be found in no other way. It is the contention of this chapter that it is there, in God, that all historical process, through which the dynamic of creation moves on in continuity and with novelty, is everlastingly treasured and employed.

Before this book ends, there are a few further considerations which may be advanced, largely by way of amplification of what has already been said. I wish to comment on what is often styled "the consummation of all things," with what the Book of

Revelation calls the coming of "a new heaven and a new earth"; the sense in which Christian faith, with its claim to specific revelation in event, is a special or (as the tradition puts it) "unique" religious position; and the significance of the "Christian hope" so far as persons in their subjectivity are concerned. The discussion will be brief, with but one or two paragraphs given to each of these matters.

First, as to "consummation." The story of the beginning of the world in Genesis is mythological; its purpose is not to give us information about some presumed moment or moments of time when the world came suddenly into existence. Rather, its purpose is to insist upon the dependence of the whole creative process on the continuing activity of God (however this is conceived). Similarly, the pictures of a "new heaven and a new earth," and all the rest of the material which talks about "consummation" or the "end" (in contrast to Genesis' concern with "beginning"), are not intended—or cannot be understood by us as meaning—a picture of how the world will "finish." Its purpose surely is to insist that God himself is the ultimate one who receives what is accomplished or achieved in the creation. All history finds its fulfillment in him, just as the history of each occasion, of each human life, finds its fulfillment there.

As there is no theological reason for believing that the creation came into existence at some given moment of time, so there is no theological reason for thinking that it will be consummated and "end" at another moment of time. We may equally speak of a continuing creation, with God always active in it and with an unceasing dependence upon him for the provision of the initial aims of all occasions. Indeed this is a *better* way of envisaging the situation, since it is hard to conceive of a Creator who does not create, a cosmic Lover who is not always actingly lovingly towards that which is not himself—and I doubt if the attempt of some theologians to provide God with an "object" of his love in the second hypostasis of the Trinity is a very effective substitute. Likewise, we may see the "consummation," if we wish to use that term, as the continuing reception by God of the achievements accomplished in the creation; a *better* way, I should say, than to subscribe to some final winding up of creation for ever.

Second, there can be no doubt that the fashion in which Christian faith is related to its originating event, both in respect to Jesus Christ himself and also to the ploughing of its response to the event into succeeding history as a positive community, is different from that taken by other world religions. The "uniqueness" is not one of separation or "exclusion" but of fulfillment and "inclusion"—the terms are Professor Moule's. Here is a vivid and decisive manifestation of an attitude toward the historical which has dim parallels, but not identical representations, in Judaism and Islam, perhaps in Mahayana Buddhism In these religions, history counts for a great deal. But Judaism does not find a focal activity of God in a total human life; it looks to its great patriarchal figures and to Moses. Islam regards Muhammed as the Prophet but not as incarnate Word. Perhaps in Mahayana Buddhism we come closest to the Christian view, but in that religion the historical figure of Gautama is important more for what he taught and for his being the great type to which all his followers are to conform, than for being in some decisive sense the expression of the divine in human event. And futhermore, in Buddhism the attitude toward the realm of happening is very different indeed from that which governs Christian thinking.

In these and other religions, as well as in other areas of human experience, a Christian ought to be prepared to grant—not condescendingly, either, but with generous delight—that God has been present and active because he is always present and active in the world of events, both natural and historical; *a fortiori* he is there in the devout faith of men. So we need not isolate the Christian faith from everything else, religious or secular; but we must claim that it can serve, in its distinctive type of historical dependence, as a completion and correction of other ideas of God. This attitude is implicit in the teaching of the patristic age and in the main tradition of Christian theology, in contrast to the narrower view which some sectarian groups have taken in their mistaken zeal for defending the Lord whom they serve.

Finally, what about the subjective participation of men in the fulfillment of history? This has traditionally been part of the great Christian hope. Does the conceptuality we have found useful in understanding fulfillment in God make any provision for this?

There is the danger of claiming too much and the opposite one of saying too little. Here I wish to distinguish carefully between what may be called the certainty and the permitted hope. When I say certainty I do not mean, of course, mathematical or logical demonstration. I mean the assurance, within the context of the Christian faith and the process conceptuality, for which I have been arguing in this chapter. Perhaps certitude would be the better word, since it does not carry the connotation of demonstrable proof. By permitted hope, I mean the confident expectation which may be a direct consequence of taking with utmost seriousness the deliverance of Christian faith itself.

The certainty or certitude is found in the concept of "objective immortality" by virtue of which every occasion or occurrence or event must make some contribution to the ongoing process and to the "consequent" nature of God—God in his concrete actuality as related to and working in the creation. If the schema which I have presented is true, or near enough to truth to be taken as trustworthy, then for good or ill the decisions made by every entity or occasion and the actions which have followed upon those decisions, at every level of the creative process, have mattered to God and have had their consequences for him. The same is true of each human life as in its distinctive fashion during its span of years it has worked for or against the purpose of love which moves through the world.

Obviously the "evil that men do" (or that anything else does, for that matter, in impeding the creative advance, diverting it, or diminishing it) cannot be "accepted" by God and received into his life, as can the good. Insofar as this evil "lives after them," to continue the Shakespearian quotation, it lives in the distortion, frustration, side tracking, and diminishment of God's purpose. If there has been good hidden in it, as surely there must have been, this can be used by him. The Cross, in itself an evil thing, became an occasion for great good because God distilled from it the good that was there: the willing self-giving of the Crucified.

But what about our subjective share in this taking of good into God? Does each conscious life lived in the process subjectively know itself to be remembered by God? In terms of the conceptuality here adopted, it may or it may not. The conceptuality does not demand it nor can it deny it. We have here what I have styled a permitted hope. If there is other reason to believe this, it is certainly permissible to do so. We may hope that in some fashion, unknown to us now, not only the good done by each personal series of occasions but also the occasions as a conscious series may become "alive in God" and a cause of delight to him as he employs the good and its agent for further loving action. This would mean that the experiencing self is aware of its reception into God's "consequent" nature, in the "communion of saints," and aware of being used by God in love for the purposes of love. The reason for this hope is primarily the victory of Christ over death, evil, and wrong—a victory validated by the historical remembrance that he was known, in his personal integrity as a man, to his disciples after his death on the Cross. At its heart, Christian faith has the conviction of Christ's Resurrection. And we may say that those who are united with him, in whatever way this occurs, are also "risen with him" and thus share with him in the life which is his in God.

But when this is said about what I have styled the permitted hope—which means not some wistful yearning but an eager expectation or yearning—it must also be said that Christian faith cannot allow a dog-in-the-manger attitude, in which any one of us refuses to make his contribution to the creative activity of God unless he can be assured of his own abiding existence as a subjective agent. Such an attitude would be entirely un-Christian.

I can hope for subjective awareness in God's "consequent" nature *only* if I see this in terms like the "communion of saints." That is, it is not something to hug to oneself; it is something which one is urgent in desire to share. It is not a matter of glory for me, but a yearning for God's glory, which is nothing other than his love in act. All love is love only when it is sharing, with others and with God. That is true in God's own nature as it is true in the world of our own experience. If I understand this, I am then permitted to hope that in some fashion beyond my present imagining I may participate with God and with my fellows in the fulfillment of history, in which has been wrought out that good which God desires. As the American Book of Common Prayer phrases it, this is "a holy and a religious hope."

So much for comment on the three matters. A final word must be said. The discussion in this book has been in terms of process. But this must not be taken to mean "progress," in the cheaper sense of that word. All too often it is assumed that to speak of the historical process necessarily includes the idea of a continuing and almost automatic improvement in the human situation, so that in a certain numbers of years evil and sin will be done away and a perfected human society will arrive. But the fact of man's possible decision against the God-intended good remains with us always. There is no automatic progress. At the same time there is the assurance of faith that improvement is not impossible, even in human affairs, and the abiding conviction that in God perfection exists and is shared, where and as and when men respond to it. In the fulfillment of history in God, the Kingdom of Heaven is realized, since God's sovereign rule is the character and quality of that Kingdom—and he is always the suffering yet triumphant Lover who takes into himself what the creation has achieved, blessing it and transforming it.